96

This book was donated
to honor
the birthday of

Laura Hachla '97

by

Cheryl and Peter Hachla

10~13~95

DATE

Fresh Ink

Fresh Ink

Behind the Scenes at a Major Metropolitan Newspaper

DAVID GELSANLITER

Foreword by Gene Roberts

University of North Texas Press

Denton, Texas

10   9   8   7   6   5   4   3   2   1

The paper in this book meets the minimum requirements
of the American National Standard for Permanence of Paper for
Printed Library Materials, Z39.48-1984.

Library of Congress Cataloging-in-Publication Data

Gelsanliter, David.

Fresh ink: behind the scenes at a major metropolitan newspaper /
David Gelsanliter.

p.   cm.

Includes index.

ISBN 0-929398-84-X. – ISBN 0-929398-91-2 (pbk.)

1. Dallas morning news.   2. Dallas times herald.   3. American newspapers –
Texas – Dallas.   4. Journalism – Texas – Dallas.   I. Title.

PN4899.D34G45   1995

071′.642812 – dc20   94-43363

CIP

Also by David Gelsanliter

Jump Start: Japan Comes to the Heartland

For my mother

CONTENTS

FOREWORD

If you had to list the deadly sins of the newspaper business, among the most deadly surely would be: (1) journalism by rote and rigid formula, and (2) purse strings so tight that they strangle a newsroom's ability to react to the news and to the diverse needs and interests of its readers.

But America's newspapers of the 1990s seem to be flocking to formula journalism and underfinanced newsrooms, although history fairly screams out against this. And for a very good set of reasons. The biggest news stories, events that rivet readers to their papers, almost always contain an element of unpredictability. You might say surprise is a defining characteristic of the truly big stories. And formula newspapers tend to bobble the big ones. Why? To make a formula work day after day, a newspaper has to weed out the reporters and editors who are most adept at throwing away the book and coping with surprise in favor of staff members who are comfortable with rules and rote. When the big story arises, the conformist staff cannot cope and the paper loses a major opportunity to demonstrate that it is dependable and readable at the very time when readers care the most.

We tend to forget, but many of our newspapers went through an orgy of formula in the fifties and sixties. Brevity was made a virtue above all of the virtues and tight restrictions were put on the jumping of stories. Some newspapers went so far as to prohibit any jumps from page one. One of them was *The Dallas Morning News*.

On November 22, 1963, President John F. Kennedy was shot within two blocks of the newspaper. You could see the assassination spot from the newsroom windows. You can guess what happened. Except on a couple of days, one of the biggest stories of the Twentieth Century was not jumped. True, there were front page "reefer" boxes referring readers to eight or ten inside pages day after day. But this simply fragmented a story that cried out for coherence. The editors were too busy getting the story covered to take all the time it would have taken to steer a rule suspension through top management.

And even if they had prevailed, it would not have mattered. They had conditioned their staff away from the multi-column narrative story – the very approach the assassination demanded. So very able reporters from *The Morning News* swarmed onto the story, beat everyone at gathering the facts, but, because of an inflexible management policy, fired the facts at the readers in bite-size chunks, like bullets from a Gatling gun. The facts were there. But coherence and readability were not. Instead of being enlightened, readers became confused.

The same rote thinking that fumbled the Kennedy assassination came within a whisker of blowing the Dallas newspaper war, which escalated sharply in 1973 when Times-Mirror, publisher of the *Los Angeles Times*, which had bought the *Dallas Times Herald* in 1970, imported new management. The new management brought in aggressive reporters and editors, increased newsroom spending, and steadily gained momentum. Victory seemed inevitable for the *Times Herald*. But there were two pivotal developments. Instead of increasing the pressure on *The News*, and refusing to give it time to recover, the owners of the *Times Herald* increased its profit flow to the central corporation. Meanwhile, on *The News*, there was a generation change in management. Young Robert Decherd, an heir of the Dealey publishing family, was placed in charge.

Showing a sure instinct for putting first things first, Decherd started a nationwide search for an editor. He recognized that the search was too important to delegate to others. He crisscrossed the country personally, talking to editors and publishers, seeking advice and names of editor-candidates. In the end, he selected Burl Osborne, a key member of the editing staff of the Associated Press. The Decherd-Osborne team reversed previous policy and went on to architect one of the nation's soundest and most solid newspapers. It loosened purse strings and newsroom thinking. It became the sole newspaper survivor in Dallas – by forsaking formula and rote and parsimony in favor of flexibility, substance, a greatly expanded news staff and newshole to serve a metropolitan area that had steadily grown more complex.

In this book, David Gelsanliter tells the story of how *The Morning News* operates, with a depth of knowledge of experience authors only rarely bring to the printed page. He speaks with an authority gained by being a key player in a newspaper war, the one in Philadelphia, remarkably similar to the one in Dallas. Gelsanliter was General Manager of *The Philadelphia Inquirer* and the *Philadelphia Daily News* at a period in which the sister newspapers were developing the strategy, built around substance, that was to lead to the defeat of the *Philadelphia Bulletin*.

I can think of no untold journalistic story more important than that of *The Dallas Morning News*. And no writer better equipped to tell it than David Gelsanliter. *Fresh Ink* is a remarkable marriage of subject and author.

Gene Roberts, *New York Times*

BEGINNINGS

The Idea

When an editor asked if I would like to write a book about a week in the life of a major metropolitan newspaper, I said I would if we could find one not merely surviving but getting stronger. One likely to set a standard in the years to come. Ideally, it would not be on the East Coast or in the Midwest, but in a part of the country likely to become more important in the years to come. It would still be in a competitive battle with at least one other paper. If we timed it right, I would be there when the second newspaper shut down and could see then how the winner met its responsibilities as a monopoly.

We considered approaching the headquarters of a chain, but I'd spent eleven years with Knight-Ridder and knew how chain newspapers operate. Often, they keep one eye cocked to see how their performance plays on Wall Street. I wanted to find an independent newspaper, still family owned or controlled. I believed the test of a good newspaper to be how well it serves its local readership.

The newspaper industry has been shrinking. Fewer than two dozen cities remain with competing daily papers. Most of the large afternoon independents – the *Washington Star*, *Philadelphia Bulletin*, and *Cleveland Press* – have fallen by the wayside, the victims of suburban growth, traffic congestion, and early evening television. In cities where a single company owns the morning and evening paper, the trend is towards merging the two into one. And in cities where there have been joint-operating agreements (an arrangement where two companies combine so competing editorial products can still be published, but under a joint business operation) the weaker, usually afternoon, papers are also going under. Recent examples include the *St. Louis Globe-Democrat*, *Miami News*, *Columbus Citizen-Journal*, and *Knoxville Journal*.

At the same time, a revolution has taken place in the television industry. Since the Gulf War, CNN has become the channel of choice for breaking news. And as more cable stations enter the market, the television audience continues to fragment. A trend to fifteen-second commercials adds to the clutter, and hand-held remotes allow the viewer to switch channels at will. Television news used to be a public service, expected to earn the networks prestige instead of profits. But as business interests have taken control of programming, the result has been the end of high-quality, low-rated documentaries. Now we have news broadcasts focused on crime, sex, and celebrities. In writing this book, my assumption has been that newspapers have the opportunity to become the nation's common hearth again, as this story of *The Dallas Morning News* shows.

A newspaper's great strength is that it is still a mass medium able to gather a set of facts and create a sense of community each day. Newspapers are a unique blend of street smarts and sophisticated technology. They offer information in a convenient format that allows readers to pick and choose, savor and save. Unlike most television news shows, newspapers can add meaning and context to the day's events. They can, if they will, serve as the one place in a community where all voices meet and are heard. Should more newspapers die, what will be lost is this capacity for bridging differences, and binding people together over place and time.

By profiling a week in the life of a major metropolitan daily, I hoped to reveal how a newspaper comes into being each day. I wanted answers to such questions as: How do stories get selected for the front page? How does a newspaper balance the needs of its readers with those of its advertisers? How do the people being written about respond to the coverage? I stuck to this format, but thanks to luck and good timing, was able to do even more.

Why *The Dallas Morning News*

The Dallas Morning News was my choice to profile because it was family controlled and had all but won the great Texas newspaper war by earlier defeating a richer, more powerful rival. In doing so, it was challenging some of the industry's conventional wisdoms.

– It put the emphasis on factual instead of interpretative reporting, and on substance rather than sizzle.

– When in doubt about a sensitive story, it often chose to wait and gather more facts rather than be first to break the news.

– For ten years, it had grown in circulation, both daily and Sunday, and its readership gains outpaced population growth.

– It seemed able to maximize advertising revenues without sacrificing editorial integrity. It ran more full-run total and classified advertising than any newspaper in the country. It had won three Pulitzer Prizes during the previous five years. (Before I was finished, it won three more.)

– And it had refused to play the Wall Street game, opting for lower profits and a long term strategy instead.

Moreover, most of the challenges *The News* faced were challenges common to large newspapers everywhere. How to improve daily newspaper readership, particularly among women. How to do serious investigative reporting at a time of skyrocketing libel suit awards. How (and whether) to serve the low income part of its market about which few advertisers cared. (In Dallas, there was the related question of how to serve the burgeoning Mexican-American population.)

I was to be in Dallas during a time when the competing *Dallas Times Herald* was sinking fast. If it failed, I knew I would be in a position to tell that story as well. As Robert Picard writes in *Press Concentration and Monopoly*, most newspapers which become monopolies fail to pass on their savings to readers and advertisers. Instead, they cut costs and raise prices, charging all the traffic will bear.

Until 1970, a long and comfortable relationship had existed between *The Morning News* and *Times Herald*. Both were locally-owned and each left the other to its respective morning and afternoon monopolies. *The News* concentrated on its role as a state-wide paper with a higher demographic profile, the *Herald* on news closer to home and of greater interest to a blue collar reader.

But in 1970, the Times Mirror Corporation, publisher of the *Los Angeles Times*, purchased the *Times Herald*. Tom Johnson, a former aide to President Lyndon Johnson, was named its executive editor in 1973. That was when the newspaper war began. Veteran reporters and editors departed from the *Herald*. A more aggressive crew, many from the East Coast, replaced them. The newcomers had no ties to Dallas or the city's traditional decision-makers. Times Mirror thought they were more likely "to tell it like it is."

The war would last for eighteen years, and for most of that time, it was a battle that Wall Street and the journalistic establishment on the East Coast predicted *The Morning News* would lose.

For although *The News* under its founder, G. B. Dealey, achieved distinction during the first half of the century, it slipped under the leadership of his son and grandson, when its editorial page turned strident and ultra-conservative. For example, on the morning of the day John F. Kennedy was assassinated in Dallas, *The News* allowed a full-page ad, paid for by the John Birch Society and attacking Kennedy, to run. Earlier, at a White House luncheon for Texas newspaper publishers, *The News'* Ted Dealey had told Kennedy: "The general opinion of the grass-roots thinking in this country is that you and your administration are weak sisters. We need a man on horseback to lead this nation and many people think you are riding Caroline's tricycle."

In the late 1970s, *The Morning News* began to improve, and improve dramatically, first under G. B. Dealey's great-grandson, Robert Decherd, and then, starting in 1980, under Burl Osborne. But because of its history and location, the newspaper was slow to achieve the national recognition its performance deserved.

The A. H. Belo (pronounced bee-low) Corporation, which owns *The Morning News*, had gone public in 1981. But ten years later, when I began my research, Wall Street still considered Belo something of an enigma. Its earning record was not the rising straight line that analysts prefer, but a jagged pattern of peaks and valleys. Still, securities analysts agreed that, for a family concern, Belo had surprisingly sophisticated management. And yes, *The Morning News* was chalking up impressive circulation and advertising gains. But Belo was still a small regional company. And Dallas was . . . well, atypical. The East Coast establishment saw Dallas as a proud but insecure city, run by and for businessmen, too often associated with an assassination, a football team, or a Ross Perot.

The journalistic fraternity was still suspicious, as well. *The News'* performance was suspect, attributed more to innovative marketing techniques than to tough reporting. Critics said the paper avoided hard truths for fear of offending somebody. *The News* might be breaking new ground in color photography and graphics, but most newspapers in the northeast were still black and gray.

In 1983, the *Columbia Journalism Review* criticized the paper's "High Profile" section for flattering the rich and pandering to business executives. In 1985, *Texas Monthly* ran a favorable profile on Robert Decherd, but concluded by saying *The News* was "too carefully designed to please. It should do more than give people what they want to hear." Two years later, Robert Decherd was featured on the front page of the *Wall Street Journal*. The paper lauded Decherd for his fighting spirit and "for starting the transformation of *The Morning News* into a newspaper of distinction." But the praise was still qualified. The *Journal* questioned *The News'* penchant for boosterism, and said: "Belo has shown it can succeed in a fast-growing market. Now it must prove itself in a region battered by the oil slump." In 1991, Alex S. Jones, then media critic for *The New York Times*, said: "Although *The Morning News* has been broadening its base, there is still a lot of tension between ownership values and those of its reporters in the newsroom."

Under Decherd and Osborne *The News* has emphasized what people have in common rather than what divides them. Other newspapers might report that Dallas has more divorces and heart attack victims than other cities its size, but these have not been subjects on which *The News* has elected to dwell.

"What allows us to be on good terms with almost everybody in the legislature," said Wayne Slater, *The News'* Austin bureau chief, "is that we're not sensational. Readers know that in any sensitive story, we'll put both sides' position high up in the lead."

"On the East Coast where people want to hear the latest unsubstantiated rumor, newspapers use more blind quotes and are more interpretative," said newspaper analyst John Morton. "Dallas is more conservative. In Dallas, readers want the facts. They want to make up their own minds."

When Dallas was battered by an oil and then a real estate slump late in the 1980s, *The News* refused to cut editorial staff or column space. Nor did it reduce any expenses related to advertising or circulation sales or service. Profits plummeted, but market share accelerated. "Darwinism at work," Robert Decherd said. "In hard times, the strong do get stronger."

In 1991, in the wake of a long recession, there was a new humility in Dallas, a new respect for resiliency. No doubt this was another reason for *The Morning News'* success. The paper had come to symbolize roots in a time of too much change, a model of restraint in a state too often given to excess. In 1992, Belo became the first Texas company to celebrate its 150th birthday.

"Just because you receive the
tip at the country club doesn't
mean you disregard it."
– Burl Osborne

Getting Started

I had never met Burl Osborne, but wrote him in March, 1991, to see if I could win his cooperation. We met five days later, then I met with Robert Decherd, and the project was soon approved.

There were a minimum of guidelines. I could talk with whomever I pleased – everyone would be urged to cooperate – and I could attend whatever meetings I chose. No one would see what I had written until after it was published. And although I stayed longer than expected, no obstacles were put in my way. I wasn't always told when sensitive meetings were to be held. But if I found out later, I was free to reconstruct from participants what had been said. Newspapers have a reputation for poking into other people's business, while being highly circumspect about their own. I didn't find this to be true at *The Morning News*.

When I began to attend the daily news meetings, I found each day different from the day before. Editors handled many more words, photographs, and graphics than eventually got printed. I tried to understand the decisions they made by monitoring their spoken and, more often, their unspoken values. I tried to ascertain whether or not editors disciplined themselves to underplay or trim stories that were at variance with the wishes of their superiors. Did reporters pull their punches and, if so, under what circumstances and why? What were *The News'* institutional taboos?

I found boldness in sports and state-wide coverage, competition and a difference in values between the "word" and the "visual" people, tension between a copy desk intent on ensuring balance and neutrality and a reporter's need to speak in his or her own voice. There was a preference for the middle-brow over the consciously intellectual, yet encouragement from the managing editor to be "ahead of the curve." Big stories often got surrounded rather than synthesized, with the result that meaning and context sometimes suffered. Readers were often given a blizzard of facts, then pretty much left to decide for themselves.

The newsroom had a family feel that softened sharp edges, but often frustrated newcomers and the more aggressive. Generations were layered and old-timers abounded, although most of the newer editors and newer reporters were from out of state. There appeared to be no "attack journalists" whom an editor could unleash to bring down a person (rather than merely exposing malfeasance in an organization or institution). I found a strong and successful commitment to hiring and promoting African-Americans; in fact, in 1991, the industry's Morris Memo said *The News*, together with *The Miami Herald*, *Detroit Free Press*, and *Seattle Times*, was doing the best job in employing minority newsroom professionals. Yet there were scarcely any women in decision-making roles, and there seemed to be genuine confusion about how to serve the Dallas area's large and fast-growing Hispanic community.

On the business side, I found *The News* to be a sophisticated operation with a close monitoring of the bottom line. Each morning at ten, company officers met around a long table to identify problems before they had a chance to fester and grow. In these daily meetings many successful competitive initiatives had been launched: the idea of diverting revenue from other media by offering a discount *only* if the advertiser commits to more space than before; in circulation, the strategy of giving the home delivery customer a later paper than the reader who buys on the street.

The daily face-to-face officers' meetings helped to eliminate turf battles between the news and advertising departments, encouraging decorum and fostering a respect for tradition.

These numerous traditions revealed other nuances of life at *The News*. When the executive editor writes a memo, he uses the same color paper (pink) that G. B. Dealey did. When a former employee dies, the flag in front of the building flies at half-staff. Retirees eat free in the company cafeteria. Reporters and photographers are discouraged from wearing jeans (or cowboy boots). Women employees seldom go bare-legged, even in the scorching summer heat. The home numbers of all senior editors are listed in the Dallas telephone book.

As the week to profile, I picked the week of November 4–10, 1991, since this was when the most important city council and mayoral election in recent Dallas history would be held. It also turned out to be the week Magic Johnson announced he had the AIDS virus, the week *The News* again postponed a controversial series that would eventually win a Pulitzer Prize for investigative reporting, and the week a corporate executive arbitrarily reversed the newsroom's strategy about how to handle a libel suit.

Four weeks later, as I was compiling my notes, the *Dallas Times Herald* suddenly closed down and announced it was selling its presses, headquarters building, and subscriber list to *The Morning News*. I then found myself rethinking assumptions I'd made, and trying to answer a whole new set of questions: Why would the *Times Herald* be willing to sell to its arch-rival? Why put nine hundred people out of work two weeks before Christmas? Why close down a newspaper during the season when advertising volume is at its peak? Hadn't respected newspaper analyst John Morton said recently that Dallas, like Houston and Denver, was a young city and one of the few places still able to support two profitable newspapers? Why would the Justice Department bless such a deal? Why hadn't there been more warning?

Which decisions before and during the week I profiled were related to the secret preparations for the *Herald*'s demise? Who had known about these preparations? Was there a connection between them and what had seemed to be excessive caution in covering the local elections?

Until the day the *Herald* announced it was shutting down, competition between the two newspapers had been fierce. Starting in 1986, the *Herald* filed lawsuits charging *The News* with circulation fraud and illegal theft of comic strips. *The News* countered by charging that the *Herald* was trying to accomplish through the courts what it had been unable to achieve competitively. In 1990, the *Herald* proposed—and *The News* rejected—a joint-operating agreement under which the two papers would merge business operations while continuing to compete editorially. Two months before shutdown, the *Herald* was still filling vacancies in its newsroom. A month before, it had led its front page with a story about Dallas' most overpaid executives, and leading the list was Belo's CEO, Robert Decherd. When he announced he was selling to *The Morning News*, the *Herald*'s publisher said he had first approached a hundred other potential buyers.

Yet when the end came, both parties were uncommonly gracious. *The News* allowed the *Herald* to publish a final edition. There was no sabotage from angry staffers, and scarcely any theft of files or computers. In a front page "thank you Dallas" box, *Herald* publisher John Buzzetta said, "Dallas is fortunate in that it fostered two great newspapers. One newspaper of great distinction will remain." The next day, many of the *Herald*'s newly unemployed carriers and circulation managers helped deliver *The Morning News* to each of the 150,000 former *Herald* subscribers.

Suddenly *The News*, with a circulation of 520,000 daily and 840,000 on Sundays, was not just the biggest paper in Texas, but among the ten largest in the United States. Previously in a league with *The Kansas City Star*, *San Diego Union-Tribune*, and *The Orange County Register*, *The News* was now larger than *The Miami Herald* and *The Boston Globe*, and was approaching the *Philadelphia Inquirer* in size. While other papers with state-wide circulations had been scaling back – the *Courier-Journal* in Louisville, Kentucky, *The Des Moines Register* in Iowa, and the *Los Angeles Times* in California – *The News* had been reaching farther out. There was talk now of beefing up its Austin, Houston and Mexico City bureaus. Wall Street wanted to know how *The News* had been able to negotiate such an advantageous deal.

I wound up staying in Dallas seven months more than I had planned. I then returned two years later for a final look. Belo owned Dallas' only daily newspaper, its dominant TV station, and a protective ring of seven suburban weekly papers that had acted to discourage further competition. Dallas' city magazine, *D*, had folded, and its weekly *Dallas Observer* had failed to grow.

It seemed to be a situation unique in American journalism.

"Many Texans want to believe the rank independence and swagger that created our folkloric traditions will somehow sustain Texas indefinitely. The reality is that Texas must become integrated with the rest of the United States and world." – Robert Decherd
"We're not a Bubba newspaper." – Burl Osborne

The Players

Newspapers place such a premium on speed and accuracy that decisions get made for reasons not often articulated. Editors finish each others' sentences. Reporters know without being told what their limits are. Taboos are understood, but seldom discussed.

This pattern seemed particularly apparent at *The Morning News*, where generations are consciously layered and people with twenty, thirty, sometimes forty years of experience can still be found in a few key slots. These veterans contribute an institutional presence and memory that influence newcomers in a variety of ways. Changes are not made lightly and, once made, seldom reversed.

"It's like being part of a family," an often skeptical metro reporter told me in a reflective moment early in my stay. "I can push the edge of the envelope. If I wasn't sure somebody at the other end would apply the brakes, I'd have to apply them myself. I'd have to do more self-monitoring. I wouldn't want to work at the *Times Herald* where whatever I wrote got put into the paper without change."

I realized if I was to do justice to my story, I needed to know more about the values of the decision makers. I needed to understand what they chose *not* to say, as well as what they did say, and why. *The News* was more of an editors' than a reporters' paper than other newspapers I had known. And since most of the recent changes had taken place on the editorial side, I was putting my emphasis there.

Here then, before looking at a week in the life of *The News* and at what transpired after the death of the *Times Herald*, are brief biographies of the major players.

When in 1974, at the age of twenty-two, Robert Decherd began to build the team that would do battle with the *Times Herald*, he was guided by a need to bring about change without alienating other family members. On his return from Harvard, he had been impressed with the quality of people he found in *The News'* circulation department. "If we have this many honest, forthright, street-smart people, who aren't afraid to speak their minds," he later remembered thinking, "we must be doing something right." He decided that whenever possible he would go with "the team on the field." The newcomers he hired, however, would come from out of state.

Decherd will say his most important decision was hiring Burl Osborne, but others who know him disagree. Second most, they say. His most important decision was the one he made to return to Dallas in 1973.

Robert was at Harvard when in November of his senior year his father died of lung cancer. Robert and his father had been close, and Ben Decherd was said to have been the ablest grandson of G. B. Dealey, who founded *The Morning News*. During World War II, he served as an aide to General Walter Krueger on General MacArthur's staff. And after the war, he aspired to run *The Morning News*. But because he was a grandson on his mother's side, and had the wrong last name, he was denied the opportunity. By returning to Dallas, Robert Decherd set out to capture the prize that had eluded his father.

At Dallas' St. Mark's school, Robert Decherd had been co-captain of the football team and editor of the newspaper the year his father served as chairman of the board of trustees there. It happened to be the same year trustees dismissed the school's headmaster for being too willing to embrace the values of the counterculture. "What I remember most clearly," Robert said, "is that my father didn't try to influence me in any way. 'Do what you need to do,' he said. 'I won't second guess you. If you have questions, make an appointment and we'll talk.'"

At Harvard, Decherd was an American History major. He covered sports and news of the school administration for the *Harvard Crimson* and, his senior year, became its president, the first Texan to do so, he is proud to say. He also worked as a correspondent (stringer) for *The New York Times*. Gordon Medinica, now at the *Times*, was a house mate then, and later an usher in his wedding. He remembers Decherd as "twenty going on thirty-five, the only one of us who didn't smoke dope."

Harvard in those years was a turbulent place. Incensed by what seemed an endless war in Vietnam, students vented their rage on the universities that sheltered them. In 1971, Derek Bok succeeded Nathan Pusey as Harvard's president, and it fell upon Decherd to write about how Bok was approaching his job.

Looking back, Decherd said Bok had served as a mentor to him. "He loved sports and, though the descendent of distinguished forebears, was the most unpompous person you could ever imagine. He had great faith in reasoned consensus, and was obsessed by a need for fairness. His own profession sought him out, and he stayed the course."

A factor in Decherd's decision to return to Dallas, rather than work as a reporter for *The Baltimore Sun* as intended, was a conviction that *The Morning News* had abandoned the principles of its founder. From 1885 until the mid-1940s, George Bannerman Dealey was the principal force and guiding spirit behind *The News*. Sent by Colonel A. H. Belo, then owner of the *Galveston News*, Dealey's charge was to start a newspaper in Dallas. This Dealey did, and in 1926 he bought the newspaper from Belo's heirs.

Under Dealey, *The News* began a tradition of promoting civic improvement. The paper championed the hiring of Dallas' first city planner, the opening of Southern Methodist University, the selection of Dallas as site for the regional Federal Reserve headquarters, the adoption of a city manager form of government, and the construction of Fair Park as site for the Texas state fair. In the 1920s, at a cost of advertising boycotts and circulation losses, Dealey led a successful fight to cripple the Ku Klux Klan. *The News* became Texas' newspaper of record and the first to adopt a modern editorial page. Dealey was the prototype of the newspaper publisher as leading citizen. Unlike other prominent Texas publishers, he was able to resist using his newspaper for the advancement of his personal wealth and power. When he died, the flag at the state capitol was flown at half-staff.

G. B. was succeeded by a son, E. M. (Ted) Dealey, then by Ted's son, Joe. But neither proved to be the newspaperman their father was. In the 1950s and 1960s, when Dallas was a hotbed of witch hunting and racial intolerance, *The News* supported the philosophies of the radical right. On the day John Kennedy was shot, Ted Dealey allowed a full-page ad to run attacking Kennedy and his policies.

Robert Decherd returned to Dallas in 1973 knowing that the trust that had allowed the Dealey family to run *The Morning News* for two generations would expire in three years. By then, Decherd and his sister would control the largest single block of shares. These might be enough to put him in line to run the newspaper if he could win support from other family members.

And so on his return to Dallas, Decherd hit the ground running. He bought a town house, re-met and married Maureen Healey, a native of Temple, Texas, who had grown up in Dallas and was at the time a media buyer with a regional advertising agency. He enrolled in *The News*' newly established executive training program.

In 1974, *The News* had a pressman's strike, its first labor dispute in forty years. Instead of manning the presses as did Joe Dealey, Jr.,

Decherd volunteered to help Richard Blum, the executive in charge of breaking the strike. Decherd worked eighteen-hour days scheduling press crews, manning phones, and running messages. *The News* continued publishing without interruption. The strike was soon broken and, as the years passed, the company became virtually union-free. Blum remembers Decherd as mature beyond his years.

Several months later, Decherd and his sister, with support from their mother, went to Joe Dealey and asked that Robert be awarded a seat on the board of directors. The Dealeys had a seat; the Decherds had a right to one too, since Robert and his sister would soon become Belo's single largest stockholder. Joe Dealey dragged his feet, but James Moroney, Jr., a Dealey on his mother's side, was supportive. Decherd's mother and Moroney's wife were close, as had been Moroney and Robert's father, Ben. The two families often vacationed together at a summer place in Winslow, Arkansas. Jim Moroney hadn't known Robert well; there was a difference of thirty-one years in their ages. But in watching the way Robert had conducted himself since returning from Harvard, Moroney was impressed.

Decherd's next move was to suggest that *The News* hire Jeremy Halbreich. Halbreich had been business manager of the *Harvard Crimson* the year after Decherd served as its president, and the two were acquaintances. Born in Cleveland, raised in Los Angeles, and the son of Holocaust survivors, Halbreich was looking for a job in advertising, circulation, or production, he wasn't sure which. He had interviewed at *The New York Times*, *Los Angeles Times*, and *The Washington Post*, but none of them had a training program which would allow him to rotate through the various departments, then to decide for himself. *The Morning News* did, and Halbreich became its first non-family member.

Halbreich said Dallas in the 1970s reminded him of Los Angeles in the 1950s and 1960s – on the verge of explosive growth. Like Decherd, he brought to *The News* a rational approach, and a practice of thinking before speaking. Also like Decherd, he quickly put down roots and became active in the community. With a young ally on board, the stage was set for Decherd to play a larger role.

If Ted and Joe Dealey were gregarious and hail-fellows well met, Robert was like his father, more reserved. He didn't hunt or fish and seldom took a drink, and there was a single-mindedness about him. He knew what he wanted and went after it. His first love was editorial so he spent the bulk of his training program in the newsroom as an assistant to the executive editor, Tom Simmons. There, he declined the office Simmons offered and, given his lack of seniority, refused a space in the company parking lot. Decherd's unassuming ways impressed reporters and helped spike a Guild organizing attempt. He gave hope to those who feared *The News* would fail to be aggressive enough in response to the challenge being mounted by the *Dallas Times Herald*.

In 1974 *Texas Monthly*, founded to bring a more aggressive style of reporting to the state, had run a cover story that showed a billy goat chewing a piece of newsprint. The headline read "Texas Newspapers: BA-A-A-D." In his article, Griffin Smith, Jr., wrote:

"Texas journalism is, on the whole, weak and ineffectual. No Texas newspapers show up on the Ten Best List of *Time* or anyone else; the popular image of the greathearted crusading newspaper defending justice and smiting wrongdoers is notoriously at odds with the Texas facts. . . . Texas may be the fourth largest state and the home of presidents, space centers, and the astrodome, but in journalism it is a backwater."

Smith predicted that with Tom Johnson's arrival as executive editor of the *Times Herald*, the situation could change. And it did. In 1975, the *Herald* converted its Saturday paper from evening to morning and tripled the number of Saturday advertising pages. In 1975 *Time* magazine called the *Herald* one of the five best papers in the South. The *Herald* began cutting into *The News'* advertising lead, and for the first time nosed ahead of *The News* in Sunday circulation. In 1977, the *Herald* began publishing a limited morning edition on other days of the week.

By then most of the men running *The Morning News* were nearing retirement. Joe Dealey wanted Joe Jr. to eventually succeed him as publisher, but Joe Jr. showed neither the talent nor the desire.

By 1978, Robert Decherd was a member of the paper's inner circle. Earlier that year he had enhanced his worth and his reputation by successfully mediating a dispute between a disgruntled family member and the men running Belo and *The Morning News*. A grandson of G. B. Dealey on his mother's side, Gordon Jackson, like Ben Decherd and James Moroney, Jr., wanted to take Belo public so his stock would be more valuable. Jackson owned enough stock to threaten the company. He didn't get along with Joe Dealey or Jim Moroney, but had been close to Ben Decherd. So Joe Dealey turned to Robert Decherd for help, and Robert was able to work out an agreement whereby the company bought Jackson out.

By 1980, when Robert was named executive vice president, purse strings had been loosened, circulation and classified had been given additional resources, and all business-side functions had been centralized under one man, John Rector, who wasn't a member of the family. The next step was to hire an editor to succeed Tom Simmons, who was retiring after forty-nine years.

By then Decherd was twenty-nine, and the decision was his. The search took him eight months. He interviewed all the candidates and checked each and every reference himself. He wanted someone energetic, someone capable of understanding business needs as well as editorial imperatives, someone with the capacity to grow beyond editor to become publisher. What he did not want was an advocacy journalist, or someone who would feel compelled to impose a personal vision, or replicate something he had done elsewhere. Most of the candidates he interviewed were "still engaged in turf battles with the bad guys on the business side of the paper," he said. Those he seriously considered were David Jones of *The New York Times*, Gene Foreman of the *Philadelphia Inquirer*, Ron Martin of the *Baltimore News American*, Stuart Looey of the *Chicago Sun-Times*, Larry Jinks of *The Miami Herald*, and Burl Osborne. Decherd kept coming back to Osborne.

Osborne was forty-two, a veteran of twenty years with the Associated Press, and currently managing editor of AP's headquarters bureau in New York. If Decherd was rational and reserved, Osborne was street-smart and visceral. If Decherd was primarily interested in Dallas and Texas, Osborne had national as well as international experience. And if Decherd sometimes gave strangers the impression of being laid back, Osborne could act like a pit bull. Yet Osborne was also said to be cautious, apt to check the depth of the swimming pool before he jumped in. Though impatient and demanding, Osborne had held jobs in half a dozen places, for relatively short periods of time, and was accustomed to "taking the hand that was dealt him." He had been responsible not just for news coverage, but also for handling complaints and investigating new technology. In Ohio, publishers with widely different philosophies had used him as a sounding board.

Born in Jenkins, Kentucky, Osborne was a coal miner's son whose father died of lung cancer, a death his son attributes to work in the mines of the Consolidated Coal Company. He had been raised Baptist, was a political moderate, and the first member of his immediate family to go to college. Never having run a newspaper, he wouldn't know what couldn't be done. Although Osborne is physically short, and Jim Moroney worried that short men can have a tendency to throw their weight around, perhaps that could be a plus, too. With Times Mirror threatening to take the *Times Herald* morning, there was no time to waste. Besides, Osborne's values dovetailed almost perfectly with Decherd's own. Osborne believed in positivism, had a preference for letting facts speak for themselves, and held a conviction that if you cut back on news space, however adroitly, sooner or later the reader will know – and the newspaper will suffer.

For Osborne, too, the partnership had great appeal. He was restless. At AP, he often worked standing up and ate lunch on the run (chicken noodle soup in a styrofoam cup). He had a reputation for surrounding a big, breaking story, but had been having trouble getting all the resources he felt he needed. Because Lou Boccardi, his boss, was more polished and talked more frequently with board members, Boccardi had the inside track on being named the next president of AP.

Several of Osborne's friends, including the AP bureau chief in Dallas, tried to talk him out of taking the job Decherd was offering. He would never last, they said. He could never be the editor he aspired to be without offending Dallas' conservative psyche and affluent sensibilities, they said. What Robert Decherd had wanted, Boccardi said later, "was not just the brightest editor in the business, but the brightest editor who could fit into the culture out there."

Osborne refused to listen. Decherd wanted better business reporting, and Osborne saw business reporting as an opportunity to excel. At AP, concerned about the hostility the petroleum industry felt towards the news media, Osborne had already enrolled in an MBA program at Long Island University. Besides, Decherd kept asking Osborne how good he thought a newspaper could be, and if he thought *The Morning News* could be transformed into something extraordinary? If so, how extraordinary?

There was one problem, however.

Once Osborne agreed to take the job, Decherd brought him to Dallas to meet Joe Dealey and Jim Moroney, the other members of the ownership triumvirate. The meeting went well, but a second meeting with Belo's two medical doctors did not. They recommended that Osborne not be hired.

The problem was that sixteen years earlier, Osborne had suffered from nephritis, a terminal kidney disease. He lived two years on a dialysis machine until a single kidney, donated by his mother, could be placed in his body. The then-radical operation was a success, but *The News'* doctors were skeptical. They questioned how long Osborne could handle a demanding new job. Yes, he appeared to have a lot of energy. And yes, he had this habit of living each day as if it were his last. But at what cost? Osborne was (and still is) slightly moon-faced from the steroids he has to take.

Decherd talked with Osborne's own doctor and with the surgeon who had performed the operation. Both were convinced Osborne could handle any job. Decherd went back to Joe Dealey and Jim Moroney and said, "The best I can make of this, it's a reasonable risk. If we have five years with Burl, I think we can take this newspaper farther than in fifteen years with anyone else I've talked with."

So Osborne was hired. In his first year, he increased the newsroom budget by fifty percent, from six to nine million dollars. He raised salaries – in a few cases dramatically – and none were cut. Except in sports, and at the Washington and Austin bureaus – which Osborne felt were being run like embassies – there were no purges.

It became the perfect fit. Decherd had an intuitive understanding of Dallas, where the power lay, and who exercised it. He knew to whom you talked and what to say in a world where young men made their marks not just through brilliance and ability, but because of who their parents were. Osborne, on the other hand, was fourteen years older than Robert. He had grown up a poor boy, had fire in his belly, and also had something to prove. Plus, he had the breadth of newspaper experience that Decherd lacked.

Decherd's next hire was Jim Sheehan as Belo's chief financial officer. After Decherd became Belo's CEO in 1987, Sheehan was named its president, chief operating officer, and Osborne's boss.

By 1980, Decherd had decided to take Belo public. The company's board of directors hadn't wanted to go public on Gordon Jackson's terms, but with the mounting competitive challenge, working capital was needed for growth, and going public would allow older family members to plan their estates.

A gruff New Jersey native, Sheehan spoke the language of the New York investment community. (With Sheehan, Moroney had worried that he might be too abrasive for Dallas.) His job would be to oversee Belo's transition from a private to a public company. He also would bring financial precision to the planning process and would "ask tough questions," said Decherd. "To prevent Burl's and my enthusiasm for spending money on the news product from spinning out of control."

In 1983, Sheehan masterminded the blockbuster "Corinthian" deal that enabled Belo to buy network TV stations in Houston, Tulsa, Sacramento, and Norfolk for $606 million. These stations generated a healthy cash flow, and Belo suddenly had the wherewithal not only to pay off its debt, but also the necessary resources necessary to defeat the *Times Herald*.

Meanwhile, Osborne hired Ralph Langer (the name rhymes with ranger), to be his managing editor and Dave Smith to be sports editor. Osborne had worked with Langer in Ohio when Burl was the AP bureau chief and Langer editor of the *Dayton Journal*. He was impressed with Langer's ability to work "non-politically in a political environment."

Langer had been a psychology major at the University of Michigan, and later an Army counterintelligence officer. He started his newspaper career as a photojournalist with an uncommon talent for blending pictures with words. He had many of the qualities Osborne lacked. For if Osborne was impatient and at times impulsive, Langer was reflective and deliberate to a fault. No shouter or pounder of tables, he has an ability to defuse tension with a quick wit. At *The News*, he is one of the few people in the building to work with his sleeves rolled up.

"If Ralph didn't exist, it would have been necessary to invent him," Osborne has said.

"Being around Burl is a unique experience," Langer replied. "He thinks vertically or horizontally, depending on his mood. In his mind he goes from one to four, and expects you to fill in the blanks. If you can't, he's not always patient with you." In their first couple of years together, the two men seemed to launch a new feature or section every week. Their goal was to have in *The News* something for every interest group.

Osborne's hiring of Dave Smith as sports editor was another matter altogether. For if Langer, hired from Everett, Washington's *Herald*, was a relative unknown, Smith was already a superstar. Sports editor from 1970 to 1978 at *The Boston Globe,* and then sports editor at the *Washington Star,* Smith, like Osborne, had a reputation for pulling out all the stops for a big story. In 1977, *Time* magazine called Smith's sports section at the *Globe* the best in the country.

Osborne saw greatly enhanced sports coverage both as a way to make a big local impact and to enhance *The News'* national reputation. The best sports writers mingled at the big events – the World Series, Superbowl, NBA Finals, and NCAA Final Four. Were Smith to dramatically improve sports coverage, the word would go out that *The News* was serious about becoming a first rate newspaper. Job applicants would flock not only to sports, but to other departments as well.

A native of tiny Crestline, Ohio, where his father worked as a railroad engineer, Smith, also a former Marine, began his career at the nearby Mansfield *News-Journal* before moving south to the *Miami News* where he would become its sports editor. A brilliant organizer, Smith doesn't have a college degree, but says maybe that helps by pushing him to try harder, as well as helping him identify with the "average man." When his writers get too technical, Smith threatens to put a glossary next to their stories: to explain what a "coffin corner" is in football or an "illegal defense" in basketball. Osborne saw Smith as a man who could turn a sleepy department around and, in the doing, set a standard for other news departments to follow.

When I arrived, Rena Pederson, the editorial page editor, was still *The News'* only woman officer. A native of San Angelo, Texas, she came to the paper in 1973 after brief stints with United Press International, the Associated Press, and the Washington Bureau of the *Houston Chronicle*. A skillful writer, she wrote in covering President Johnson's funeral that he "was mourned by a crowd so silent you could hear the steel bound wooden wheels of his funeral caisson roll on the cold streets. . . . The sun was so bright the watchers shaded their eyes with their hands, and it looked for row after row as if they were offering salutes."

At *The News*, she covered the federal courts and radio and TV for ten years before volunteering to write editorials. An article she wrote for *Congressional Quarterly* criticizing the "trickle down philosophy" of Dallas business leaders caught Robert Decherd's eye. He was impressed with her understanding of Dallas and liked her easy writing style. He suggested she be made editorial page editor. Her mandate has been to moderate, diversify, and make less preachy the part of *The Morning News* which has been slowest and last to change.

PROFILE OF A WEEK
NOVEMBER 4-10, 1991

Monday, November 4

A low, gray and beige building four blocks southwest of the mirrored glass towers of downtown Dallas houses *The Morning News*. It faces a shaded park the newspaper helps maintain, where live oak trees are fitted with wire "hair nets" to prevent birds from nesting and soiling the sidewalk with their droppings. On three sides of the building are polished metal maps of Texas with a star marking the city of Dallas. A cornerstone reads, "This institution dates from 1842 when Texas was still a republic." Above the front door, in chiseled stone letters a foot and a half high, are the words of G. B. Dealey, *The News'* founder:

Build the news upon the rock of truth and righteousness. Conduct it always upon the lines of fairness and integrity. Acknowledge the right of the people to get from the newspaper both sides of every important question.

Inside, in the newsroom, there is the normal bustle and chaos as deadlines approach. Although this is the week voters are to elect the largest and most diverse city council in Dallas history, the week *The News* hopes will put an end to three years of shouting matches and infighting at City Hall, editors are taking care to appear scrupulously neutral.

In Monday's paper, there is little that is new, apart from four pages on the Cowboys 27–7 victory over the Phoenix Cardinals–and fourteen and a half pages of other sports news, nearly half of it in small type agate. Except in sports, there is seldom much breaking news on a weekend, and yesterday was no exception. Today's front page is replete with updates, advances, and enterprise stories that didn't make the big Sunday paper.

Monday's is the week's smallest newspaper, the one advertisers favor least. In Dallas, as in most cities, the heaviest shopping days are Thursday through Sunday; *The News* sells fifteen per cent more papers on Friday and Saturday than it does on other days of the week.

On today's front page are six stories and three color photographs, the dominant photo an 8½ by 9 inch shot of Cowboys' running back Emmitt Smith scoring a touchdown from the one yard line. Leading the page are a pair of stories from *The New York Times* and the Knight-Ridder Tribune service that cancel each other out. The KRT story, datelined Madrid, says Arab-Israeli negotiators fail to agree on the time and site for future meetings. The *Times* story says hopes for Mideast peace grow despite problems. Balance is a priority here, I soon learn.

On the right side of the page but still above the fold is an advance by City Hall reporter David Jackson on tomorrow's elections. Stories on 1A normally run four to seven inches and then are continued inside, as is Jackson's. At *The News*, however, often the more interesting (and controversial) parts of a story are found in the continuation, or jump. This struck me as odd, since I'd thought a newspaper story, different from a magazine article, has to grab you in the first few seconds; otherwise you turn to something else. But apparently readers have been trained to know that *The News* will take care not to be provocative. In Jackson's story, the new news is buried inside in the jump. On Sunday, several prominent African-Americans had charged that one of their number "sold out" by endorsing mayoral candidate Steve Bartlett.

On the left side of the page is a story by Austin bureau chief Wayne Slater, titled "Richards' support in poll slips." Slater writes that the Governor's support hasn't slipped very much and is still higher than what her two predecessors enjoyed. I find out that the story is on page one because an earlier page one story had said Richard's support was at an all-time high.

Below the fold is an anniversary piece by Frank Trejo on the Immigration Act of 1986. The carefully balanced headline reads "Out of hiding: immigration reform brings peace to many, but critics question its effectiveness." The story runs to seven inches on the front, seven columns inside, and is accompanied by three related stories (sidebars) and graphs. Missing, however, is any estimate of the number of "undocumented workers" in the Dallas area. It was not possible to get an accurate estimate, Trejo explained. Nor, apparently, did the Hispanic metro editor encourage him to do so. At *The News*, reporters use the phrase "undocumented workers"; editorial page writers say "illegal aliens."

Above the masthead in magenta is a line promoting the weekly science section, "Discoveries." "Advances in prenatal diagnosis, page 6D," it reads. A box at the bottom of the page refers readers to a story inside about the police shooting of a seventy-year-old man after he "clicks" a pistol at them and refuses to drop it. Although crime rates in Dallas are among the highest in the nation, *The News* seldom puts crime stories on its front page unless they are illustrative of a trend.

"News is what happens at the margins of our lives," Burl Osborne explained. "We see our newspaper as a member of the family – coming into the house before breakfast, before you've had your first cup of coffee, when you may still be a little grumpy. Tone of voice is important then. There is seldom a need to shout."

Today's front page, like all front pages at *The News*, is colorful. It features a dominant photograph, two smaller photos and graphs, and a block-by-block modular makeup which tends to the horizontal. Special attention is paid to the cutline under a photograph, since surveys have shown that the first thing a reader looks at on a page is the lead photograph. Cutlines have high readership, second only to headlines. On a *normal* day at *The News*, headlines are all pretty much the same size. In Dallas, where most readers drive to work rather than take public transportation, screaming headlines – like those employed increasingly by the *Times Herald* – aren't thought to sell newspapers.

The weekday paper has five news segments: a first or "A" section, a Metropolitan or State section (depending on where the papers get sent), a Sports Day section, a Today (lifestyle) section, and a Business section. Each of these has a full color front. On Wednesday, a Fashion ! Dallas and a Food section are added, and on Friday, Guide (entertainment) and House and Garden sections.

Today's Discoveries section was once self-contained, but it is now part of the Business section because it did not generate enough advertising support. Its front page, like the front page of all soft (or feature) sections, is designed on Macintosh computers by the art department. Today, multicolored graphics explain medical breakthroughs, what acid rain is, and how earthquakes happen.

In scanning today's paper, managing editor Bob Mong finds plenty to criticize.

Mong rises early, tries to run three miles before breakfast, and reads four newspapers (his own, the *Dallas Times Herald, New York Times*, and *Wall Street Journal*) before starting his work day around nine.

An Ohio native with a Quaker background, Mong came to *The News* in 1978 after driving halfway across the country at the suggestion of a friend in Forth Worth who thought Robert Decherd might be on the verge of creating something special. Decherd soon convinced him to be the paper's new business editor.

Nicknamed the "obscure genius," Mong is a big man with an impassive face who, despite several promotions, still drives a battered white 1986 Nova. His definition of a good reporter is "someone who can ask tough questions in a matter-of-fact way, is fair-minded but not soft, straightforward but not coy, and able to shift gears if the story is not what he or she thought it was."

Today, in notes to executive editor Langer and executive managing editor Bill Evans, he writes "we badly overplayed" a story on the Metro front about "the hole experience; body piercing on the cutting edge of pop culture. It should have been edited more carefully. We should never have made it a special report. Serving our readers needles through the nipples is beyond belief." The color photograph accompanying the story showed teenagers wearing nose and ear rings. The nipple rings weren't mentioned until the sixth and ninth paragraphs.

Mong also blames himself for a story that led the Today section titled "Tight times in the Park Cities: whether pawning the Rolex or buying used designer dresses, even the affluent are feeling the pinch." This one, he says, hit all the clichés. "I got an advance copy and plain forgot to read it."

The Today section has become a place where editors put stories and features that won't fit anywhere else: essay-like lifestyle pieces; health and fitness features; music, movie, and television reviews; personal advice columns; consumer complaints; the horoscope, crossword puzzle, and two full pages of comics. Editors have begun to fear that the section doesn't meet the needs of the woman of the 90s.

Next, Mong tells deputy managing editor, Stu Wilk, that the *Times Herald* had two stories over the weekend which *The News* missed. Wilk oversees the metro, state, and business departments and, when necessary, bypasses assistant editors and talks directly to reporters. He came to *The News* from the *Milwaukee Sentinel*, by way of the *National Enquirer*. There, he says, he learned ways to convince people to do things they don't want to do. He and Mong have a good guy/bad guy relationship with the staff, with Mong often perceived as being above the fray. As *The News'* lead over the *Times Herald* has widened, the two have had to battle complacency. Veteran reporters often prefer to work on stories of their own choosing rather than cover the routine events a newspaper of record is obliged to chronicle.

Meanwhile, on the fourth floor above, Rena Pederson is meeting with her editorial writers and her cartoonist to plan the week ahead. Three of the seven are former reporters and three have come to the paper from Washington think tanks. One is African-American, one is Hispanic, and two are women.

The petite, impeccably dressed Pederson reports to Osborne, who hadn't had any experience with an opinion page before coming to Dallas. At AP, he was trained in a school where the important thing is balance, and opinion is steamed out of the copy. As the *Times Herald* continues to lose readership, Osborne has become more insistent that *The News'* editorial pages be balanced.

"When there's a mix of voices, if we make a mistake, it's not as damaging," he said. "People have other alternatives they can turn to. But if we're essentially alone, tone of voice becomes critical. If we're seen to be consistent and fair, even those who don't agree with us will listen to what we have to say."

Pederson copes by being chatty and conversational, as in this recent column:

"Question: What's the difference between Atlanta and Dallas?

"Answer: Atlanta just won the global beauty contest to become site of the 1996 Olympics. Dallas didn't even try.

"Atlanta is assured of being the boom town of the 1990s. Dallas is still having an identity crisis.

"Back in 1987. . . we suggested Dallas put together a commission to compete for big league sports events. Great idea, said city leaders. But then came the usual list of reasons why not to bother: Times are hard. The business community is in a daze. The minority leadership is confrontational rather than cooperative. It's too hot. There's no mass transit system. The Cowboys can't win. Waah, waah, waah."

And she has responded to Osborne's need for greater balance by running editorials that list first the facts, then a "yes" column next to a "no" column. Finally comes "our view," as in:

"Conundrum: Should college students be given prophylactics?

"Our view:

"We don't think condom distribution is an appropriate activity for high schools, the problem of teen pregnancy notwithstanding. . . . College campuses are another matter. But at the same time there must be greater effort on the part of college officials to encourage the examination of lifestyle questions within a moral context as well as a health context."

On being named editor of the editorial pages, Pederson banned use of the words liberal and conservative. *The News* has since supported a state income tax, gun control, and the hiring of gay police officers. While remaining conservative on money issues, the paper has campaigned against alcohol abuse, and opposed both the playing of religious music by school marching bands and the constitutional amendment that would punish flag burning. *The News* now endorses Republicans and a few Democrats for local and state-wide offices, but since 1940 has endorsed only Republicans for president. In 1964, the paper remained neutral in the contest between Lyndon Johnson and Barry Goldwater.

Today, standing before her blackboard, Pederson asks Richard Estrada what he thought of today's story by Frank Trejo on immigration. Estrada is *The News'* immigration expert. Born of Mexican-American parents, Estrada spent his formative years in the Panama Canal Zone, where his father was stationed as an Army officer. He has said that, growing up, he was occasionally mistaken for black, and perhaps as a result is often perceived as more sympathetic to Dallas' African-American community than to its Mexican-American one. He is the former research director for the Washington-based Federation for Immigration Reform (FAIR). Like FAIR, he is in favor of drastically reducing even legal immigration, and is an outspoken advocate of tighter controls along the U.S./Mexico border.

Estrada didn't much like Trejo's story. He says Trejo should have emphasized the need to close the loophole of counterfeit documents. Only then will employer sanctions against hiring illegal aliens be effectively enforced.

Pederson nods, pauses, but then says we've made that argument before, and moves on. She admits to thinking about tomorrow's election. She has already run *The News'* endorsements three times and set up a hotline so readers can call in if they need to be sure. She and her people have interviewed all six mayoral candidates, several more than once, and at least fifty candidates for city council. She has agreed to run letters favoring or opposing candidates until election day so long as the charges aren't frivolous or unanswerable, such as "so and so sleeps with pigs." She and associate editor Henry Tatum will be in on election night to write commentary for Wednesday's paper. And she hopes the message will be "It's a new day for Dallas," not "Uh-oh, they're back again" (a reference to the most divisive of the incumbents).

At meeting's end, Tatum says he has put together a page of letters in response to the Peirce Report. The Peirce Report, an analysis of Dallas' strengths and weaknesses, has been *The News'* attempt to place tomorrow's election and the issues facing Dallas—its north-south split, shrinking tax base, and fractious city council—into larger perspective. A half million people live in south and southwest Dallas, most of them African-American or newly arrived Hispanic, and the region has become an economic disaster area.

Osborne commissioned the report because he thought that at this juncture, a sophisticated outsider could give his readers the necessary context more credibly than his own people could. Titled "Defining the future: In 2010 will the city of Dallas be dynamic or decaying?" the report ran as a self-contained section nine days before the election. It was written by syndicated columnist Neil Peirce, urban specialist Charles Johnson, and two Texans—an African-American woman and a Hispanic man. They had spent ten days in Dallas the previous June interviewing sixty community leaders selected from a list of 200 provided by *The News'* editors. Peirce had previously done similar reports for papers in Phoenix, Seattle, Baltimore, and in Owensboro, Kentucky, where Osborne sits on the newspaper's board of directors.

The report had two scenarios. The "worst case" showed freeways becoming further ensnarled, the city center moving northward, and Dallas's north-south split intensifying as the city experiences an American version of apartheid. By 2010, Dallas could be sixty-two per cent Hispanic, Peirce said, and could elect its first Asian-American mayor.

The best case scenario showed what the city could be like if it garnered the courage to elect a strong mayor, capable of convincing a larger, more diverse city council to abandon tactics of grandstanding, especially when the television cameras are whirring. Tax revolts would be inevitable, Peirce wrote, if voters got the idea that council members spend money on pork for their districts rather than for the good of the whole. An African-American middle class must be encouraged to develop, and African-Americans must learn to cooperate with the faster growing Hispanic community.

The original version of the Peirce Report predicted that race riots could occur at North Dallas shopping centers if the city didn't overcome its north-south split. Osborne asked Stu Wilk to delete that part of the report, but not the part predicting the large increase in the Hispanic population by 2010.

At 10:30 each Monday, sports editor Dave Smith sits with his three assistant editors and critiques the Saturday, Sunday, and Monday papers. He goes through the sports sections page by page, column by column, in a search for the misleading headline, the page of "boring gray type" unrelieved by a graph or photograph, or the story, paragraph, or sentence even that the *Times Herald* or *Fort Worth Star-Telegram* carried and his people missed. His assistants have learned to rise early and read the papers as carefully as their boss does. They know if they can anticipate and deflect his barrage of questions, they will get fewer ulcers. They welcome me at these meetings because they say my presence softens the attack.

"If somebody makes a mistake and says I feel really bad," Smith explains, "I say 'it's good that you feel really bad. Now don't worry about it.'"

He admits he's hardest on his editors (he often praises his reporters and columnists, rewarding them with silence when displeased), since he's training them to be sports editors themselves one day. Many have left to do just that. Sports editors at the *Fort Worth Star-Telegram*, *San Antonio Light*, *The Orange County Register*, *The Baltimore Sun*, and *Chicago Sun-Times* are all Smith-trained.

Smith came to *The News* in 1981, and within months had won over Texans by doubling coverage of high school sports, Southwestern Conference football, and hunting and fishing. He added more writers to those already covering professional football, basketball, and baseball. And he started giving year-round coverage to local golf tournaments, bowling, horse racing, rodeo, and cycling events. Nicknamed "Mr. Agate," he believes the way to hook both hard-core and casual readers is to put in the Sports Day section everything from how many points the neighbor kid scored in a basketball game to the results of downhill skiing in France. In 1991, sports accounted for twenty-five per cent of total news space and seventeen per cent of the professional staff at *The News*, a total of thirty writers, fifteen copy desk people and five editors.

In 1978, John Rector and Robert Decherd had asked the research firm of Yankelovich, Skelly and White to do a study of *The News'* strengths and weaknesses, compared with those of the *Times Herald*. Results showed the *Herald* to be winning in virtually every category, including sports and business, where the morning paper should be dominant. Yankelovich had never seen a market where there was such an intense interest in sports, however, or one in which so many well-educated people took no newspaper at all. *The News'* advantages were limited to its upscale demographics, a more reliable distribution system than the *Herald*, and the morning advantage it had thus far failed to exploit. When Osborne arrived in 1981, he made enhanced sports coverage his first priority.

Smith is in a better mood today than usual, although he tries not to show it. "We should have had a separate story about the three NFL games won Sunday with a Hail Mary pass," he says. And he complains that photographs from Sunday's Cowboys' game were too tightly cropped. Professional sports don't generate as much emotion as do college sports, and Smith likes to create excitement with photographs that show crowd faces or more of the action.

Sports uses more photographs and graphics than other departments, and until recently both the photo editor and art director had reported to Smith. Given Smith's reputation as a "kick ass" kind of guy, Osborne thought his section could set the standard. But as several photo editors and art directors burned out, Ralph Langer took photography and graphics out from under Smith's control. As a result, other departments became more visual. When Smith was in charge, he had specialists covering every sport. But now photo editor John Davidson is rotating his shooters, as they are called. Davidson says rotation adds freshness. Rather than the wide angle shots that Smith prefers, Davidson often asks for something closer, an elbow thrown or a facial expression you can't get on instant replay. (Davidson, after receiving a political science degree from the University of Missouri, served in Vietnam as leader of a reconnaisance patrol, often behind enemy lines. Like Smith, he has a short fuse. When the two men disagree, Langer often has to mediate.)

Smith sent four reporters and two columnists to Phoenix to cover the Cowboys/Cardinals game and, apart from the photographs, he can't find fault with the coverage. He is especially pleased with the work that Cowboys beat writer, Rick Gosselin, is doing.

Gosselin says he doesn't use a tape recorder because he listens better when he doesn't. Nor does he pad his copy with quotes, talk to star players like Emmitt Smith or Troy Aikman unless he really needs to, or attempt to bother coach Jimmy Johnson at home. After Gosselin criticizes a player, he makes sure he's at practice the next day to take the heat. And since in football, unlike baseball or basketball, it can be hard to see what really happened, especially on defense, Gosselin usually waits until he's talked with a coach who has seen the game film before assigning blame. Gosselin has a Cowboys story in the paper every day except Friday, when somebody else fills in. And he keeps all his own statistics, including many not kept (or released) by the Cowboys: dropped passes by player, catches of over thirty yards and under ten, quarters when quarterbacks are most and least efficient. Jimmy Johnson has told Smith that Gosselin knows as much about football as most NFL general managers do.

Smith is high on the Cowboys. Unlike the area's other two pro teams (the baseball Rangers and basketball Mavericks), the Cowboys generate excitement. And unlike some veterans on his staff, Smith prefers the Jimmy Johnson/Jerry Jones style of Cowboys football to what he experienced of the Tom Landry/Tex Schramm era. Schramm acted as if he owned the media, says Smith. He thought he could dictate what was written about the team. As a way of fostering dependency, he refused to cash the checks Smith sent to pay for food his people ate in the press box. Johnson, in contrast, came in and opened the place up. He tore out the maze of cubicles in the locker room and got close to his players. Johnson doesn't care what color a player is so long as he gives 110 per cent. Under Johnson, the Cowboys aren't patient and methodical anymore, but entertaining.

And Smith thinks sports should be entertaining. He's an unreconstructed hometown fan. He says he can't remember a Texas reader ever calling to congratulate him about exposing a scandal. Like most editors at *The News*, Smith returns each and every phone call he gets from complaining readers. Stories about gambling and drug abuse in sports should run in other sections of the paper, he believes. He has a reporter assigned to do investigative work, but gets impatient if a project takes more than a week to complete. Smith's emphasis is on saturation coverage of what happened yesterday in all the essential details.

At *The News*, as at most newspapers, sports writers have more freedom: freedom to express an opinion, to use an interpretative lead, even to say things that elsewhere in the paper might be considered taboo. When the Texas Rangers were debating whether to move to Dallas or stay in nearby Arlington, for example, and *The News* was saying on its editorial page they should move to Dallas, sports columnist Randy Galloway urged the Rangers to stay in Arlington. Arlington was offering the better deal, he said. And when tennis star Monica Seles dropped out of Wimbledon, columnist Cathy Harasta wrote that her failure to explain could be interpreted as PMS syndrome. Earlier, Harasta wrote in a column titled "So-so players usually worst with women," what it feels like to be a woman in a NFL locker room. "It helps to practice the same relaxation techniques learned in natural childbirth classes," she wrote. "Focusing intently on some spot on the ceiling makes the situation bearable."

Osborne agreed that giving sports writers such freedom is a "philo-sophical loose end. But the sports section is different," he said. "If a sports writer says something outrageous all I hear is 'Oh, there goes Galloway again.' But if someone from Metro or Business does it, I hear *The Morning News* has taken a stand."

At noon Monday, the Dallas Citizens Council is holding its annual meeting in the ballroom of the Fairmount Hotel, and *The Morning News* is well represented. Belo has a table near the dais, Robert Decherd is giving one of the three speeches, and two of the three past or soon-to-be-elected Council presidents are members of Belo's board of directors.

The Citizens Council was the 1937 brainchild of R. L. "Bob" Thorn-ton, a developer who coined the phrase "keep the dirt flying." Com-prised of CEOs and captains of industry, the Council was the motor that created a modern Dallas. The construction crane became the official city bird and Dallas touted itself as the Swiss watch of Ameri-can cities, the last urban bureaucracy that really worked. Million-aire businessmen were elected mayor after serving as head of the United Way, the Civic Opera, or Park Board, and City Council mem-bers were elected only after securing the Citizens Council's blessing. Dallas boasted of never taking federal funds, and of never having had a race riot.

The Citizens Council had helped Dallas avoid the bruising racial battles of the 1960s by desegregating the city's restaurants and public accommodations virtually overnight. But because the integration was mandated by a small group of white businessmen in collaboration with an even smaller group of African-American leaders, pent-up anger in the community never got adequately expressed. Civil rights battles in Dallas often seem twenty years behind the times. The Citizens Council's philosophy of emphasizing building projects had worked well when it came to mobilizing support for a world-class airport, downtown library, or convention center, but far less so in meeting the needs of the city's underprivileged.

The Citizens Council began losing its clout in the 1970s when courts began striking down the at-large system of electing City Council members. It lost more clout in the mid to late 1980s when many Dallas companies went bankrupt or were sold to outsiders. New CEOs had less time to devote to public affairs.

At the City Council, first had come the 8-3 system of council representation, with eight members elected from individual districts and three, including the mayor, elected citywide. Then came 14-1 when in 1991, a federal judge ordered a system of fourteen individual districts, with only the mayor elected citywide. By then, the recession of the late 1980s had sapped most of the business leadership's political vitality.

The 1990 census showed Dallas to be a majority/minority city – twenty-nine per cent African-American, twenty-one per cent Hispanic, and two per cent Asian. The African-American population had stabilized, but the Hispanic and Asian populations continued their rapid growth. Robert Decherd and *The Morning News*, fearful that a 14-1 plan would bring Chicago-like ward politics to Dallas, had advocated a more gradual approach, Decherd with a contribution from his own pocketbook.

In today's speech, Decherd calls for a renewal of the city's infrastructure by tapping all possible sources of state and federal funds. Although few such funds are available now, the speech has a symbolic importance. Tall and still boyish looking at forty, with short hair and horn-rimmed glasses, Decherd later acknowledges that, like G. B. Dealey, he has a passion for city planning. He calls it a hobby, but it is obviously more. It was Decherd who convinced *The News* to hire David Dillon, a former SMU professor and Harvard Ph.D., to be its architecture critic. The three foundations he administers – Belo, *The Morning News*, and WFAA-Channel 8 – contribute heavily to new concepts of urban design.

Each weekday at 2:30, editors meet in their third-floor conference room for the first of two discussions about what will be on tomorrow's front page.

The conference room is small, tucked between the glass-enclosed offices of the five senior editors and the open expanse of cluttered desks that make up the metro department. On two of the walls are eighty plaques and framed certificates commemorating the prizes *The News* has won since Osborne arrived. Most are local or state-wide in nature, although two of *The News'* three Pulitzers are there, plus a disproportionate number of awards for photographic excellence. On the third wall hang Saturday, Sunday, and Monday front pages. The room's only window faces a driveway and Belo's WFAA – Channel 8.

No daily decisions are more than important than those about what to put on tomorrow's front page. *The Morning News*, like *The New York Times*, is a newspaper of record and its editors' goal is to give readers a broad sampling of the most important news each day. Since national and international editors don't have sections of their own, their stories often receive preference on page one.

The News had a Mexico City Bureau before Osborne came. It began expanding other international coverage in 1985 when temporary bureaus were opened in Toronto, Tel Aviv, and Managua. Permanent bureaus were then established in Bogota and Berlin, with a satellite office in Moscow. Osborne's idea was to do something else that the *Times Herald* couldn't or wouldn't do. When the recession hit Texas, the *Herald* had reduced editorial space, so *The News*, by expanding its international coverage, heightened the contrast between the two papers, and created an impression of adding bulk. "A newspaper without a good international report is like eating unleavened bread," Osborne said.

Presiding at today's 2:30 meeting is William Wilson (Bill) Evans, the executive managing editor. An Oklahoma native, Evans came to the paper in 1956 and, like many of the veteran editors, started on the copy desk and worked his way up. Besides presiding at the daily news meetings, he handles most reader complaints, relations with production, and he symbolizes the institutional presence. His style is folksy and inclusive. When Langer came to the paper in 1981, he made Evans his principal assistant. He says Evans' intuitive sense of when a problem in the newsroom is brewing has saved him many a headache.

To Evans' left sits managing editor Mong and to his right Stu Wilk. Down the table are ranged the national, foreign, state, business, and news editors, and behind them the metro editor, city editor, and representatives from Sports Day, the Today section, photography and news art. Langer usually attends these meetings, and is there today. However, he always sits in the back, near the door, and seldom speaks until at the end of the meeting. Langer, Evans, and Mong make up the triumvirate of senior editors and try not to step on each others' toes.

The meeting starts after editors hand out summaries of stories they have ready or that their reporters are working on. Hard news offerings usually do better than soft at these meetings.

The Today and business editors seldom push stories for page one because they believe their best work gets better display on a section front than when placed (or in their parlance "buried") below the fold on 1A.

Connected by speaker phone is G. Robert Hillman, who runs the Washington Bureau on a day-to-day basis, and is its primary link with Dallas. This arrangement leaves Carl Leubsdorf, its chief, to concentrate on matters of larger concern. Leubsdorf is the former chief political officer for the Associated Press, and was the third of Osborne's initial hires.

Hillman says he has a strong story by White House correspondent Kathy Lewis on the Reagan presidential library opening. Five former presidents will be there with their wives, and photography says it will have pictures of them. News art is preparing a locator map and chart showing what's in the museum.

Mong notes that polls are calling the Pennsylvania senatorial race between Dick Thornburgh and Harris Wofford a toss-up, and asks how Hillman plans to cover it. Hillman says out of Washington, since the bureau is short-handed. Because President Bush prefers to be associated with Texas, rather than Maine, and has surrounded himself with Texans, *The News* is accompanying the President on all his trips. Both Leubsdorf and Lewis are covering the White House. This strategy has resulted in better access for a regional paper, but has stretched an already small Washington staff thin.

National editor Ed Dufner says he has a toxic waste story from Ohio that fits in nicely with *The News'* environmental concerns. It was written by metro reporter Todd Copilevitz, who grew up in nearby Pennsylvania. Every couple of weeks a reporter from a different department is assigned to the national desk to write a story or stories of his or her choosing. It's a way to evaluate talent, a motivational tool, and a chance for less experienced reporters to get exposure on page one.

International editor Jim Landers proposes a story from George Rodrique in Moscow about a dissident priest. Rodrique, a former Pulitzer Prize winner, is the most experienced of *The News'* foreign correspondents. The story has been on Landers' desk for a week, and now looks like a good time to run it since on election day page one needs to be kept low-key and non-controversial.

Landers worked as a journalist in Saudi Arabia before being hired by *The News* as its first energy reporter. He talks with his foreign correspondents by phone several times a week, and each day faxes them a list of stories the national and metropolitan desks are working on, plus a list of stories that make page one. This way they know what their competition is and are less likely to get frustrated at delays in getting their stories published.

State editor Donnis Baggett proposes an election preview summarizing Texas-wide issues on tomorrow's ballot. The two most important are a lottery that supporters say will eliminate the need for a state income tax, and a billion dollar bond issue to build more prison cells. *The News* has supported both on its editorial page, the lottery reluctantly.

Business editor Cheryl Hall says she has two good stories, but prefers to run them both on her section front. One shows how local companies are grappling with the parental leave issue, the other that Dallas home prices are falling. Metro editor Gilbert Bailon says he has an election advance predicting weather and turnout. Representatives from the visual side of the paper report on the various photographs, maps, charts, and fact boxes they are preparing.

Evans reads off a list of stories that at this point he considers worthy of page one, and nobody disagrees. Mong and Langer ask to see copies of the falling home price story, Wilk of the parental leave story, and the meeting adjourns.

At 4:30, when the group meets again, Wilk has rejected the parental leave story because it's written too much from management's point of view, Mong and Langer the homeowner's story because the price declines are too small. Bailon reports that metro is chasing a report that a toddler has been found starving in a Fort Worth suburb. And a wire story has come in saying Congress has rejected the biggest overhaul of the nation's banking system since World War II. These stories will also make page one.

Thus, by early evening the front page is pretty much set. News editor Walt Stallings checks his computer terminal to see what the *New York Times* is putting on its front page, in case he might have missed something. Then he reads all the stories on each of the hard news fronts, paying special attention to the "A" and Metropolitan sections, where stories are likely to be the most controversial. He scans the photographs and graphics and checks each headline for accuracy and tone. Another editor monitors CNN, and a third editor the ten o'clock news on Dallas' three major TV stations. Stallings seldom remakes the front page or the metro front for a late breaking story, however. When the competitive war was raging, he often did, but now the philosophy is that it is better not to rush a sensitive story into the paper unless you're sure. On late-breaking stories, a short item is usually tucked inside as a brief. If the event is important enough, the story is fleshed out the next day.

"It's the difference between a paper anxious for the scoop and intent on winning the battle, and one concerned with winning the war," says city editor Rodger Jones, who used to work for the scrappy (but now defunct) *Columbus Citizen-Journal* in Ohio. "It takes a lot of self-assurance to wait and be sure before breaking a big story."

Stallings oversees the news desk where stories, photographs, and graphics are arranged on the page, as well as the universal desk where stories get a final edit after leaving their desk of origin. At papers like *The Washington Post*, the originating desk has control over which stories go where on a section front. But not at *The Morning News*.

"Decisions about coverage need to be long term," Osborne explained. "Consistency is critical to reader loyalty. Putting something in one week and slipping it out the next won't impress anyone. A page with hard news headlines one day and soft magazine features the next will only make readers wonder if you know what you're doing."

An often cited reason for *The News'* success has been a concern for credibility. Editors take care to discourage reporters from shooting from the hip.

"We have been long accused of being too colorless or boring because of a policy of avoiding pejoratives or stereotyping adjectives," said Langer. "Yet if anything has brought us as far as we've come, it's the perception that we're neutral, that we don't choose up sides, that we don't have a smartass, patronizing attitude. A reporter doesn't have to be weird to be creative."

If a person faces a grand jury investigation, and the jury later dismisses the charges, *The News* is careful to print the dismissal story on the same page, in the same position on the page, and with the same size headline. When the Texas legislature mandated a three-to-two ratio of women's to men's toilets in new public buildings, the headline in the *Times Herald* read, " 'Potty parity' bill to offer women welcome relief"; in *The News*, "House approves restroom parity bill."

A routine story passes through at least one editor on the desk of origin (sometimes two), plus a copy editor, then a supervising editor. Any sensitive or accusatory story goes also from writer to projects editor, then to all or most members of the senior management group (Wilk, Mong, Evans, Langer, and occasionally Osborne). A legal opinion, if appropriate, is sought at this point.

After senior editors leave for the day, Stallings will call Bob Mong if he has a question about how or where to play a story, Bill Evans if he needs a later deadline or to add pages to a section, Ralph Langer if he thinks a headline might be libelous, or if something moves on the wire that could affect *The News* or Belo as an institution.

Stallings leaves the building between one and two in the morning, after the last update has been made to the last edition, and the last approved copy sent to the composing room. From the composing room, page facsimiles are sent by fiber optic cable to *The News'* new printing plant in Plano, twenty-five miles away.

A Fort Worth native, Stallings came to the paper after graduating from the University of Texas at Arlington. Like Bill Evans, he started as a copy boy and worked his way up. When his friends say he's lucky to have worked for only one company, he tells them they're wrong. Two companies, he says. Before Burl, and after.

Stallings sees himself as his newspaper's last line of defense. He has a slow and deliberate walk. In the newsroom, they call him "the ice man."

Tuesday, November 5

Tuesday begins with breakfast at eight in the Beau Nash room of the Crescent Court Hotel.

In attendance are city manager Jan Hart, publisher Osborne, executive editor Langer, and editorial page editor Rena Pederson. The hotel is a convenient place to meet since three of the four live in North Dallas, and the Crescent Court is between their homes and offices downtown. (Langer lives on Lake Ray Hubbard, twenty-five miles to the east.)

Meetings with the city manager are a ritual repeated more or less quarterly. Senior editors also meet regularly with the mayor, police chief, FBI agent-in-charge, Mexican consul general and the CEOs of American Airlines, Texas Instruments, J. C. Penney, and Electronic Data Systems. There is seldom a set agenda for these meetings. The goal is to explore topics of mutual interest and to ensure that should a crisis occur, the lines of communication will be open. *The News* also has separate groups of economists, energy experts, employers, and teenagers with whom its editors regularly consult – further examples, if examples are needed – of how *The News* monitors and stays close to its community. Editors at most newspapers meet periodically with community leaders, but *The News* has developed the practice into an art form.

At this morning's breakfast meeting, Osborne does most of the talking. He is on edge, concerned about today's City Council election, and about the deterioration in civilized political behavior overall.

For the past several months, county commissioner John Wiley Price has been sporadically picketing Belo's Channel 8 and *The Morning News* next door. Price's grievance is against Channel 8 for failing to give African-American staffers enough air time. But since Belo owns both properties, Price often extends his picketing to include *The News* building as well. *The News* has gone out of its way to train and promote African-Americans, and Osborne obviously doesn't appreciate being singled out this way, although he won't say so directly.

At this breakfast, he says he fears Dallas is in danger of becoming another Chicago or Cleveland, one step away from a ward system in which members of City Council will be more concerned with their own narrow interests rather than with the good of the whole. Pederson notes that one candidate has already said his first concern will be to make sure his district gets one-fourteenth of the pie. She expresses the fear that newly-elected council members will bypass the city manager and deal directly with department heads. What can be done to restore a tone of civility in council meetings, Osborne asks. Aren't there rules that can be better enforced? What if Diane Ragsdale gets re-elected, someone else asks. Ragsdale, the African-American *mayor pro tem*, recently got into a shouting match with supporters of white police officers. The incident, replayed on national television, has become a symbol of the image Dallas wants *not* to portray.

What about the collective bargaining agreement the Dallas Police Association wants, Osborne wants to know. And the deterioration of downtown? Is it likely that Fina and Mobil Oil will move their office headquarters elsewhere? What about Neiman Marcus?

Hart is Dallas' first woman city manager, promoted into the job two years ago. She has nineteen years of experience at City Hall, and theoretically all the power. Neither the mayor nor the council members have the right to tell department heads what to do without first going through the city manager. The problem is that when the city charter was written, no one expected to be faced with such a large, unwieldy, and potentially disruptive council.

Hart tries to be reassuring. She says she thinks most of the turmoil is over. Of the four big cities with a council-manager form of government (Dallas, San Diego, San Antonio, and Phoenix), Dallas is the last to go to all single-member districts. Other cities haven't had problems adjusting. She doesn't think Dallas will either.

Yes, she says, there are things a new mayor can do to ensure more decorum at council meetings. The necessary rules are in place. And yes, work is underway to convince Fina, Mobil, and certainly Neiman Marcus to stay downtown. She doesn't think a collective bargaining agreement is necessary, or desirable, given police chief Bill Rathburn's communication skills. But she does go out of her way to defend Diane Ragsdale. Diane is one of the most hard-working and conscientious council members. What you see of her portrayed in the news media is only a tiny fraction of who she really is. But yes, Diane does have a temper.

The meeting illustrates the fine line that *The News* treads between attempting to run, or set an agenda for, the city, and ensuring an impartial news report. At the breakfast, executive editor Langer says nary a word.

At nine each weekday morning, Bill Evans meets with production director Jimmy Correu, circulation manager Darrell Martin, and Tommy Sandoz and Jerry Dunn from retail and classified advertising. Sometimes the talk is about whether there were late ads that required filler copy in the early run, sometimes it's about reproduction problems or whether sports will need a later presstime for West Coast game stories, and sometimes it's just an opportunity for men who have been meeting like this for years to drink coffee and swap rumors about what the *Times Herald* is doing.

Today, its purpose is to double-check plans for tonight's election run. Six extra printers have been hired from the pool of part-timers to handle the heavy copy flow. And four presses instead of the usual three will be used so that the second and final editions can be combined. This way, all but the 37,000 papers destined for West Texas, Southern Oklahoma, and eastern Louisiana (less than ten percent of the run) should contain election results. To prevent a bottleneck of late copy, the national and international desks have agreed to earlier-than-normal deadlines. Several blank (free of advertising) pages have been reserved so election stories can be bunched, making them easier for readers to find. Since there will be less time for editing, the length of each story has been pre-determined so each can be trimmed from the bottom if necessary. And circulation has agreed to a fifteen minute later press off time. This is a rare concession, since home delivery by 6:30 A.M. or earlier on weekdays, and by 7:30 A.M. or earlier on Sundays, is often cited as a reason for *The News'* success.

By 9:15, before Evans returns to the newsroom, managing editor Mong has already sent a note to news editor Stallings congratulating him on making a silk purse out of another poor news day.

Dominating today's front page are color photographs of five U.S. presidents and another of their wives, wrapped around Kathy Lewis' account of the Reagan Library opening in Simi Valley, California. Titled "A tribute to the Reagan years," the package continues inside for a half page where Lewis' words are accompanied by a locator map, highlights box, and photographs of two Kennedy children who also attended. The story is rich in the texture and gossipy detail often missing from page one stories: of how Jimmy Carter was convinced to come, of which Reagan children weren't invited, and of how the affair became a symbolic celebration of the end of the Cold War. Later, Lewis said that had she had the time – and been able to find a graceful way to do it – she would have liked to have added that, on this occasion at least, Reagan seemed more in command of himself than in his later White House years.

Mong also sends a note praising two reporters on the business desk: Tom Steinert-Threlkeld for his piece on the lessons computer executives can learn from a CEO's ouster at Houston's Compaq company, and Diana Kunde for her story on how local companies are dealing with the parental leave issue. Kunde's story is accompanied by a four-color graphic.

Mong has been critical of business news lately. There are too few details of conflict, too few looks beneath the surface to discover how decisions are made, too many stories being written from a single source, and too many others that are overly technical and hard to read. During the recession many Dallas companies were bought by outsiders, and *The News* is not as plugged in as it used to be.

The Yankelovich survey had singled out business news, like sports, as a potential *News* strength. The *Herald* might have the momentum, along with a better reputation for improving itself, but business leaders still saw *The Morning News* as politically more compatible. In 1980, after Mong launched Business Tuesday, Yankelovich did a follow-up survey. Tuesday had been chosen over Monday because there weren't any stock tables on Monday. To add heft, local banks and savings and loan companies were charged the retail rather than the more expensive national advertising rate, and already ad volume had doubled. The new survey showed Business Tuesday to have strong support.

"It is Dallas and Texas business news that we can't find anywhere," said one CEO. "And it's indispensable. I'm glad we're finally finding it in *The Morning News*."

"I've wondered for years why the *Wall Street Journal* acts as if the Sun Belt doesn't exist," added another. "Now we don't need it."

Respondents to the new survey urged that *The News'* business coverage be further expanded, so shortly after Osborne arrived, he made it a daily feature. He had Mong give its section front a harder, newsier edge with a column of briefs down the side. Stories were written at a more sophisticated level than in other parts of the paper, and business reporters were paid somewhat more than other reporters and urged to develop a specialty. The goal was to encourage CEOs to tell their subordinates that *The News'* business section was essential reading.

Between 1980 and 1991, the business desk had doubled in size to include a staff of sixteen reporters, four copy editors and six editors. In contrast to sports, it has had little turnover in personnel. Recent surveys had shown one of the section's best read features to be a daily column by forty-one-year veteran (and former city editor) Robert Miller. Miller puts lots of local names in his column, and tells which people from which companies are volunteering to do what. Today, he is urging readers not to forget the annual Obelisk Awards luncheon, where twenty-eight companies are being recognized for their contributions to the arts. Also in the paper today, as part of the metropolitan section, is a two-page report called Education Extra.

Launched in response to complaints that *The News* was devoting too much space to sports and not enough to academics, it features a noteworthy school, classroom teacher, or administrator each week. Today's lead story shows how college coeds can take responsibility for their own safety. An achievers column lists the names of national science scholars, and of school custodians given Apple of the Month awards by Positive Parents of Dallas.

At 9:30, the first of three weekly news management meetings is held. Attending are the three senior editors, deputy managing editors Dave Smith and Stu Wilk, eight assistant managing editors (AMEs), and two veteran staff assistants, both former line editors. Two members of the group are women and three are African-Americans. Neither the photo editor nor the art director are AMEs, and thus they don't attend. Langer and Evans speak for the visual side of the paper.

The meetings seldom last more than half an hour and have a bulletin board-like quality. They offer an opportunity to critique Saturday, Sunday, and Monday front pages and, as Langer says, "to discuss anything anybody knows that the rest of us need to hear about." Langer, who presides, doesn't appreciate being caught by surprise.

Younger members often complain that these meetings don't offer much of an opportunity to critique big decisions or to discuss journalism with a capital J. Sports editor Smith, projects editor Howard

Swindle, and Sunday editor Melissa Houtte occasionally enliven things.

Smith will complain that the front page is too dull, or too predictable, or will say more should be done to promote the wealth of good stories inside the paper. Swindle will urge senior editors to write fewer memos. "When editors behind glass sneeze, people out in the newsroom tend to get pneumonia," he says. Houtte, who soon after this week left to become editor of *D* (for Dallas) magazine, would argue for more stories written from a woman's point of view: "Killings heighten women's fear of being stalked by an estranged husband or jilted boyfriend," for example. Mong frequently brings statistics to show how Dallas and Texas are changing.

Also under discussion is whether to describe people as whites or Anglos. German-Americans have complained that the word Anglo is inaccurate and pejorative. The decision is made to say white.

How many stories should be on page one is another frequent topic. Today, the consensus is six, occasionally seven. When someone argues for more, Langer and Evans note that a photograph or graphic becomes meaningless if reduced from three columns to one. "We never consider reducing a story's type size," they say.

Most discussions center around fairness issues, with Evans, who handles *The News*' daily corrections and clarifications feature, taking the lead.

Evans and Mong say editors should have taken a closer look at a story titled "Burying the evidence: few autopsies sought in bodies pulled from the lower Rio Grande." The reporter had all her facts; the story was, in *The News*' terminology, bullet-proof. But Mong says it was marred by gratuitous embellishments.

"The corpses were photographed, stuffed into body bags, and dumped *without ceremony* in hastily dug graves. . . .

"As *usually happens* with bodies found along the lower river authorities . . . *simply assumed* that the two men had drowned swimming. . . .

"Mr. Villarreal acknowledged *with a shrug* that the victim could have been murdered and the bodies should have been autopsied. . . .

"Some . . . investigators *blandly* dismiss the corpses as those of people who drowned accidentally and never belonged in the United States anyway."

The message is: the stronger the story, the fewer adjectives or adverbs you need.

At today's meeting Smith is still upset about the too close cropping, and lopping off of feet, on Monday's football pictures. And he wants to know why, with the NBA season starting, most of the photographs from Dallas Mavericks games have been of players chasing loose balls. "Why not mix it up a little?" he says. "Why not show Rolando Blackmon taking a shot? Or Terry Davis pulling down a rebound?"

Langer, who is known to dislike "hairy armpit" photographs, grimaces. He asks Smith if he has discussed his problem with photo editor John Davidson. Smith has not.

At 1:45, the first of several planning meetings for the big Sunday paper are held. All departments are represented and Walt Stallings presides.

He goes around the room once, asking each editor what projects his people are working on, then a second time to ask which of these stories are, or could be, ready for Sunday. Metro editor Bailon has a feature titled "Hooked on Phonics" that looks promising. International editor Landers has another story from George Rodrique in Russia. Projects editor Swindle says the controversial "Abuse of Authority" series is about ready to resume. No one suggests any follow-up to today's election results.

Likewise, at the 2:30 news conference, there is little discussion of election coverage beyond assurances that all bases are covered.

Pre-election coverage has been wide, if not deep. Editors have tried not to be controversial. Each council district has been profiled, and each of the fourteen council races awarded a story, but by a different reporter so there are scarcely any comparisons or attempts to ascribe meaning. All press conferences and most of the candidate forums have been covered, and whether incumbent or unknown, each

candidate has received the same number of paragraphs. There has
been no detailing of campaign finances or any but the merest mention
of who is behind this or that candidate. The same policy holds true
for the mayor's race. Each candidate was awarded a profile, all of the
same length, even though three of the six had no chance of winning
more than a handful of votes.

Only rarely – in a piece by political writer Lawrence Young about
the willingness of gays and lesbians to endorse candidates for the first
time, and in a page one story by Lori Stahl on the values of the three
leading mayoral candidates – has any attempt been made to place what
is happening in some larger context. This obviously had been the role
of the Peirce Report.

Stahl revealed that Kathryn Cain had picketed in Berkeley against
the Vietnamese War; that Forrest Smith, the son of a union man,
had worked for Mobil Oil for thirty years before becoming president
of the Chamber of Commerce; and that Steve Bartlett, the runaway
leader (endorsed by *The News)* had at the age of twelve organized
support for presidential candidate Richard Nixon. Of Bartlett's opinions, she wrote, "the occasional angry outbursts of council members
are a problem in themselves. To his rivals, such clashes are merely
'symptomatic of the city's belated social changes.'" Stahl, a Dallas
native, the daughter of a former City Council member and previously
on the police beat, pushes for and is occasionally allowed more lee-
way. Lawrence Young, an African-American from Los Angeles soon
to be moved into a sub-editor's job, had been cautioned to be less
aggressive in his reporting.

The News' strategy was to publish all the information that was
readily available, then to let readers decide for themselves. Each
reportorial conclusion, however innocuous, had to be attributed to a
named source. Editorial control reached such a point that metro editor Gilbert Bailon said he felt his reporters could scarcely write "The
sun came up today" without adding "according to the U.S. weather
service." Two weeks before the election, Bailon met with copy desk
editors to complain that they were neutering his copy.

A native of Tucson, Bailon had come to the paper from the *Los*

Angeles Daily News, by way of the *Fort Worth Star-Telegram*. When his reporters and editors have questions he can't answer, he often convenes departmental meetings, invites senior editors to attend, and encourages his people to ventilate. It saves time, he said. He has a rubber stamp in the shape of a cow that he uses on memos received from senior editors before passing them on to his assistants.

Bailon thought that in their election coverage his people were being held to higher standards than were reporters on the state and national desks. He was right. The city edition (home final) is what Burl Osborne reads. "The closer to home any story is," Osborne explained later, "the more important microscopic details become, the more sensitive people are to any minor inaccuracies, perceived slights, or imbalance."

Reporters at *The News* chafe at the restrictions they are under, but seldom become unhappy enough to quit. Turnover rates are lower than in the industry as a whole. They are lower because *The News* has continued to improve and expand, because reporters are given weeks, sometimes months, and occasionally years to finish a project, and because the newsroom pays well.

Salaries are on a par with those at *The Boston Globe, Chicago Tribune,* or *Philadelphia Inquirer,* once cost of living differentials are factored out, said Ralph Langer. News reporters say that chain newspapers are more bottom-line oriented, and as a result the competition there is more cut-throat. Save for plagiarism, employees at *The News* are almost never fired. "You can make a mistake here and it's not fatal," said Vernon Smith, an assistant managing editor who came to Dallas from *The Detroit News.*

"We're putting together a product that blends tomorrow with yesterday," said Osborne. "You lose people with an institutional memory and a creative sensibility and you pay a high price."

"The difference between working one place all your life and being with a chain where you stay for two years, then go to another city, is that for a lot of us this is home," said state editor Donnis Baggett, a native Texan and sixteen-year veteran at *The News.* "For some people, it may be easier to be a crop duster, to drop your load and move on. Then you don't have to deal with the natives."

Craig Flournoy, a veteran reporter and another Pulitzer Prize winner, agreed that this time *The News'* election coverage had been unusually cautious. But he added that he had never written an investigative story that didn't make the paper, or had a tough story significantly watered down, or had any prominent names in a story removed.

The News endorsed five African-Americans and two Hispanics for the enlarged City Council, but among them were neither of the two black incumbents, nor any of the men or women who had fought for fourteen single-member districts. Instead, the African-Americans and Hispanics that *The News* endorsed were relative unknowns who didn't bear the scars of previous battles, or they were people who had demonstrated an ability or desire to move into the middle class. The vote by *The News'* editorial board was not unanimous, however, just as it had not been in a previous decision to endorse Clayton Williams over Ann Richards in the gubernatorial race. *The News* has no provision for making its internal dissent known to its readers.

"We felt the city needed as many new council faces as possible," said Robert Decherd, who sits in only on interviews with some of the mayoral, gubernatorial, and presidential candidates. "Most of the incumbents, including most of the white incumbents, had gone past the point of being constructive."

The News endorsed all but one of the seven white incumbents, however.

At 10:00 each morning, *The News'* officers meet around a long table in the former Belo board room. To reach the place you have to pass through a smaller room which serves as a museum and memorial to G. B. Dealey. Dealey's three desks and his filing cabinet are there, and prominently displayed is the motto he insisted on hanging throughout the building: "Be gentle and keep your voice low."

There is seldom an agenda at these meetings. The men are in shirt sleeves and Pederson in a dress and hose. No one is required to speak, and usually several elect not to. The meeting's purpose is "to find problems before they find you" and to identify opportunities. While the newspaper war was raging, these meetings gave *The News* a competitive edge. "If we wanted to try something new, we'd have to go back to the mother ship in Los Angeles for approval," former *Times Herald* editor Will Jarrett later admitted. "It sometimes took weeks for us to get a response. Whenever *The News* saw an opportunity, they could turn on a dime."

Believing they couldn't win without dominance on Sunday, *News* executives used their 10:00 meeting to make a quick decision to launch a (Saturday afternoon) Sunday bulldog edition. Later, when they heard the *Herald* was about to phase out its afternoon circulation in Plano, within hours they had tripled their circulation sales effort there.

The 10:00 meeting evolved from an experiment begun in 1978 by Joe Dealey. If the presses were late, causing home delivery to be late, circulation director Frank McKnight would arrive looking for the culprit, then usually fire off a memo to advertising director Harry Stanley. But by the time the memo reached Stanley's desk, he had usually gone to lunch. Joe Dealey got the two men to meet face-to-face every morning, and gradually, other officers joined in.

Today Jeremy Halbreich, whose title is president and general manager of *The News*, sits at the head of the table and presides. Known for his good manners and ability to draw people out, he is the meeting's calm rudder. All the business-side executives report to Halbreich. Halbreich, Langer, and Pederson report to Osborne who, when not out of town or across the street at corporate headquarters, sits in one of the chairs at the end of the table. "If this were more of a political organization," he said, "it wouldn't make sense for me to let Jeremy preside. But this way I can be more reflective. I can pick my spots."

Controller Barry Peckham passes out a flash report that shows revenue and expenses against budget for the month and previous year. Since expenses are under budget and revenues only slightly behind, there is no discussion. Harry Stanley, the senior advertising vice president who learned his newspapering at the Louisville *Courier-Journal*, asks Rena Pederson if she thinks Diane Ragsdale will win today's council race. Pederson shrugs and says Diane has an organization capable of turning out a big vote. Circulation director Frank McKnight is next. He started at *The News* in 1950, fresh out of high school, and seldom talks very much, telling me that when he does, it sounds too much like bragging. Today, though, he allows that he's heard the *Houston Chronicle* is down 16,000 in Sunday circulation, which means *The News* is now number one in Texas. Halbreich offers congratulations. Then Osborne mentions he will be on the East Coast Wednesday through Friday, and asks if he can meet later in the day with Peckham and financial vice president Bill Cox to review next year's budget preparations.

Osborne will be meeting Wednesday in New York with members of the Pulitzer board, and on Thursday and Friday in Miami with board members of the American Society of Newspaper Editors (ASNE) and with the program committee of the American Newspaper Publishers' Association (ANPA). He has been asked to put together a panel discussion on the subject of "Journalism vs. Marketing: Where do you draw the line" for ANPA's annual convention. The question of how to maximize advertising support without sacrificing editorial integrity has become one of the industry's hottest issues.

Since Osborne arrived at *The News*, its executives and editors (and by 1994 two of its reporters) have held leadership positions in nearly all the leading newspaper trade associations. Osborne served as last year's president of ASNE, Langer is this year's president of the Associated Press Managing Editors' Association, Peckham has been president of the financial officers' association, Harold Gaar of the marketing association. The list goes on and on.

Before Osborne left AP, Keith Fuller, its president then, advised him to get involved in association work. "You can see the influence and advantage the big chains have," Fuller said. "How great their potential voting strength is. But if you are willing to do the committee work, to do whatever is asked of you, your company can have an impact on a par with the chains. That's because when the votes are taken, they're taken in secret. And most newspaper people vote their professional ties before their organizational ones.'"

In getting himself and his people involved in association work, Osborne's objective originally was two-fold: to put *The News* on the map ("how can we be a newspaper of distinction if nobody knows who we are?"); and to learn as much as possible about other papers' competitive strategies. Now there was a third objective: to know and be known by potential sellers of newspapers. By 1991, Belo aspired to be more than a single-newspaper company. Editors and business executives were being stockpiled at *The News* with this goal in mind.

The 10:00 meeting adjourned at 10:27. Afterwards, advertising executives Harry Stanley and Rick Starks met with Ralph Langer to discuss a potential problem between advertising and the newsroom. If an advertiser complains about a news story, Starks will first find out if it contained any inaccuracies and whether or not it was timely, before making a complaint. If Langer is proposing to overload the advertising department's favored "A" section with stories that might be postponed or could fit elsewhere, Stanley may attempt to dissuade him. Rather than have such delicate issues dealt with by middle managers, they are handled at the officer level in the interest of avoiding turf battles.

When Osborne met that afternoon with Peckham and Cox to review next year's budget, he found projections to be within $150,000 of where he had hoped. Although the Texas economy was still in the doldrums, *The News* was adding fourteen full-time people (including four in the newsroom) to its complement of 1727. Department heads, aware that other Dallas companies were still laying off, had held costs down to existing levels, after subtracting out extraordinary expenses from coverage of the Gulf War.

The News had sent four men and two women reporters and a photographer to cover the war, resulting in a cost overrun of half a million dollars. But the gamble paid off. For the six-month period during which the war was on, daily and Sunday circulation doubled their normal two and four per cent growth rates. Supervised by international editor Jim Landers, *The News* had emphasized the war's Texas connection. Much of the advanced weaponry was built in Texas, and close ties had existed between Texas and the Gulf since oil was discovered in the Middle East. Special editions were published the first two days of the war, and again when it looked as if Iraq would accept a Soviet-brokered peace offer. State desk reporter Lee Hancock made American hostages her beat, focusing on the families of Texans held captive. Houston bureau chief Bruce Nichols profiled New Waverly, Texas, a town of one thousand, with two dozen soldiers in the Gulf. And typically, *The News* strove for balance. George Rodrique later talked about being assigned to a pool of reporters aboard an aircraft carrier:

"Perhaps we got too close to the people we were living with. One pilot told me, off the record, that they easily spotted Iraqi tanks at dusk. The Iraqis left the tanks' turrets exposed to sunlight all day. The heat they stored made the metal turrets beacons to the aircrafts' infrared sensors as the surrounding sands cooled. If the Iraqis covered their tanks, they'd be much more difficult targets. I didn't print that but read about it a few days later in *The Washington Post*."

In a speech to the American Society of Newspaper Editors, Osborne said:

"In the battleground of public opinion, the press was clobbered in the Persian Gulf. . . . Many people believe the press didn't care about the safety of their sons and daughters and wives and husbands, and that the press was arrogant (as usual), and ill-prepared and out of touch with the values American soldiers fought to protect.

"The fact is that the American people believed that strict controls on reporting, including censorship, were appropriate and necessary. And the fact is that we, the press, failed to persuade people that timely, first hand reporting will, in the long run, best serve the public interest, and that we do understand the need for military security."

Tuesday night, the Dallas Mavericks were playing their third game of the season and second at home. They had already suffered a blowout at the hands of the Spurs in San Antonio and an overtime loss to the Los Angeles Lakers, playing without an ailing Magic Johnson in the opener. If they didn't win tonight, they would drop to a 0–3 start for the first time in club history.

Four years before, the Mavericks had been more popular in Dallas than the Cowboys. They reached the Western Conference finals and seemed poised for a run at the championship. But then came a spate of bad luck and worse personnel decisions, and their most talented player, Roy Tarpley, was banned from the league for drug abuse. In 1991, what little remained of pre-season enthusiasm had evaporated when the Mavericks' management failed to sign Doug Smith, their top draft pick, until after training camp began. When Smith finally did report, he was overweight and out of condition. Erich Schlegel's photograph today shows Smith bent double trying to catch his breath as coach Richie Adubato looks on in exasperation.

Dallas has little patience with losers, and as beat writer Mitch Lawrence had written in *The News'* basketball preview, "The Mavericks are seen by a lot of people as sputtering." Lawrence and coach Adubato are close, however – because they both grew up in New Jersey, because both are excitable ethnics in a Waspy town, and because Lawrence, like Dave Smith, believes poor management, not coaching, is the Mavericks' problem.

Lawrence has been at *The News* for seven years, and has followed the Mavericks for four. Before the Mavericks, he covered SMU sports, and before coming to Dallas, professional football. He prefers basketball. "Baseball players are usually high school graduates from small towns in the south. Pro football is regimented and militaristic, with access to the players strictly limited. Basketball is a city game. The players are sophisticated, articulate, nearly all college graduates. You spend eighty-two games with them – at home and away – and after the first month or so, there are no secrets left."

Tonight, Lawrence has on jeans and the blue blazer Dave Smith insists he wear when sitting on press row in view of the crowd. Coaches wear suits, assistant coaches wear sports coats, and Smith has this thing about his people looking professional. While still competing with

Bob Mong for the managing editor's job, Smith unsuccessfully proposed a dress code for the entire newsroom.

The Mavs are losing again and Lawrence concentrates. He looks for something, for anything that might suggest this season won't be another disaster. He focuses on Doug Smith's three minutes of playing time. Forty seconds into the second quarter, Smith nails Cleveland's Craig Ehlo with a forearm to the sternum. Smith is whistled for a two-shot foul. The act shows Smith has a mean streak, one of the reasons Adubato wanted him, Lawrence writes. Smith's mean streak might be something to remember from this otherwise forgettable night.

Meanwhile, two hundred yards away from Reunion Arena in *The Morning News* building, election results are coming in. With more than half the vote counted, Bartlett is winning in a landslide. In the council race, six of the seven white candidates are winning, as are two of the minority candidates *The News* chose *not* to endorse – veteran incumbent Al Lipscomb and Chicano newcomer Domingo Garcia. Four other minority candidates, including Diane Ragsdale, appear to be headed for runoffs.

By 10:30, most election stories have been filed. Different reporters covered the mayors' race, the council race as a whole, each of the fourteen individual council races, and each of the major issues on the local and state-wide ballots. Thirty-two staff-written election stories, twenty-five photographs, and nine charts, briefs boxes, graphs, and locator maps will appear in tomorrow's paper. But apart from a story on page 30A by Lawrence Young, there is no analysis to speak of, just the bare results.

Quoting a consultant to back up each conclusion, Lawrence says Bartlett ran a textbook perfect campaign. Bartlett contended that anyone who criticized his congressional record was guilty of negative campaigning. He reminded voters that criticism only contributed to the turmoil, shouting, and name calling he intended to put an end to at City Hall. And he outspent his opponents three to one (still no mention of where the money came from). Young later revised his story to include a sampling of representative precincts. The sampling showed Bartlett to have won with seven out of ten white votes, four out of ten Hispanic, and one out of ten African-American.

The revised story made what is called the "fly," (late changes made to the final edition after the presses start rolling). It would reach readers in North Dallas where few Hispanics and fewer African-Americans live. The headline, "Bartlett's race never stumbled," remained unchanged.

Wednesday, November 6

Dominating Wednesday's front page is a 6 by 6 inch color photograph of mayor-elect Bartlett dancing with an Asian-American campaign worker, as if to suggest strong minority backing. The cutline reads "Bartlett won with 54 per cent of the vote, avoiding a runoff despite facing five opponents."

A column listing final results of all twenty-three local elections runs down the left side of the page and a facts box gives similar results for the thirteen propositions on the state-wide ballot. A second box lists by subject and page number twenty-nine election stories to be found inside.

Flanking the photograph are the four most important election stories: "A big win for Bartlett: run-off for mayor unneeded," "Council to have record number of minorities: Rags-dale in run-off," "Houston votes out [mayor Kathy] Whitmire," and "Wofford overwhelms Thornburgh in [Pennsylvania] upset." Inside, on page four, is a story that otherwise would have been on the front page: "President Bush cancels trip to Far East; faces growing pressure in economic, domestic policy at home."

Although final election results are summarized graphically on page one, many of the stories inside are still hedged, as in "with most of the votes counted, Dallas voters were rejecting a measure to allow police to negotiate pay and benefits." And although it is obvious that in two of the five majority black districts, white or white-supported challengers have forced a runoff, nowhere is this specifically stated.

Typically, the *Times Herald* is more blunt.

The editorial Rena Pederson wrote last night says, "it's a new day for Dallas."

"Steve Bartlett scored a resounding victory by sticking to the simple message that he can bring positive change. . . . He kept asking voters if they were satisfied with what has been happening at City Hall. . . . He promised to put an end to the bickering that has kept the City Council from resolving problems. . . . He promised to use his experience as a congressman to win needed federal support. . . . He promised to keep the pressure on major banks to loosen their purse strings and start investing in the inner city [read South Dallas]. And he promised to be the city's best salesman in the tough battle for corporate relocations."

In an adjoining column, Henry Tatum reminds readers that the mayor was the only official elected by the total community. Tatum urges council members to begin thinking about coalition building.

On the sports front, legendary columnist Blackie Sherrod laments the Cowboys' uninspired victory over the Phoenix Cardinals Sunday.

"Now no one is accusing Johnson's group of being a great team. Most see it, and have seen it since summertime, as a break-even outfit at best. . . . But if a great team can win games on its bad days, then a pretty good team can win games on its pretty bad days. . . . If there is a Sunday on the last half of the schedule when Dallas could afford to have an off day, it was against Phoenix. If they repeat that humdrum act against any other team from here on, they will return with their heads under their arms."

At seventy-two, Sherrod is the dean of Texas sports columnists. He left the *Times Herald* to join *The News* after columnist Skip Bayless defected from *The News* to the *Herald* in 1982. Smith didn't try to keep Bayless. "Nothing against Skip," Smith said in an interview with *D* magazine. "He's very talented. But his concern was with Skip, not the [*News'* sports] section."

Sherrod tends to be philosophical; Bayless, at the *Herald*, is more visceral.

By 10:00 in the morning, KLIF's radio talk show host Kevin McCarthy has stopped fielding calls about the election and turned to lighter fare. McCarthy thinks *The Morning News* takes itself too seriously. Today, in his weekly satire on the paper's Park Cities edition, he reads, to the music from Dragnet, from its police and fire report: "In the 4300 block of Belclaire, vandal threw pumpkin through glass storm door; in the 2900 block of Rosedale, thief took lawnmower from garage; in the 3900 block of Amherst, vandal threw egg on BMW in driveway."

Highland Park and University Park, called the Park Cities, are known as "the bubble." They are to Dallas what Beverly Hills is to Los Angeles or Coral Gables to Miami – an enclave of tree-shaded streets and stately homes where socially prominent rich people live. They are communities within the city privileged enough to have their own school system, police and fire departments. Although the previous generation of *Morning News'* owners and executives lived in the Park Cities, Robert Decherd, Burl Osborne, and Jeremy Halbreich have elected not to. They live in nearby north Dallas instead.

In 1989, *The News* created a once-a-week special section for the Park Cities. It did so after the launch of far more ambitious sections for Plano in Collin County, twenty-five miles to the north. Owing to the success of the Plano edition, the Park Cities, because of their self-contained government and many small retailers, seemed to offer an ideal site to test further zoning. With North Dallas and Plano, the Park Cities are part of the third congressional district, the state's wealthiest, and one of the most affluent congressional districts in the nation.

The third congressional is the district Steve Bartlett represented for four terms before he returned to Dallas and ran for mayor.

Unlike newspapers like the *Chicago Tribune* and *The Miami Herald*, *The News* had been slow to embrace zoning. It was expensive, it was time consuming, and it was hard to motivate reporters and ad salesmen to give as much attention to a fraction of their newspaper's press run as they would to the whole. *The News* saw (and still sees) itself as the unifying voice of its region, and didn't want to encourage fragmentation. The Dallas area is young and still relatively homogeneous. It doesn't have many mature suburbs with distinct personalities. And apart from the seven weekly newspapers ringing the city that Belo owns, there are few competing newspapers or shoppers in the area. Besides, the *Dallas Times Herald* had tried zoning, and failed.

The opportunity in Plano, however, was too tempting to resist. Plano was in the third fastest-growing county in the country, and had already attracted the corporate headquarters of J. C. Penney and Frito Lay. Plano had the potential to be more than a suburb, and *The News* was building its $160 million printing plant there. Plano's business leaders, dissatisfied with their hometown paper, the Harte-Hanks owned *Star-Courier*, came to *The News* asking for help. By then, the North Texas economy had soured, and executives at *The News* feared that further rate increases could force many of their smaller advertisers out of the paper. Zoning would be a way to retain small advertisers and perhaps gain additional circulation as well.

Thus, Plano was selected as the first site for a zoning experiment. A survey showed residents to be homebodies who wanted a community bulletin board and more news about neighborhood crime. In 1987, special Thursday and Saturday Plano sections were added to *The News*, and within a few months they had generated enough advertising to show a profit.

The sections contained a mix of spot news and human interest stories, a wealth of color photographs and an "Inside Plano" column. The column, its editor made clear, would answer questions about the city but not "provide responses to complaints about businesses or institutions." Inside was a police blotter alphabetized by street, a map showing frequency of crimes by location, and a listing of births at the hospital and new books at the library. Sports got big play, featuring everything from church league basketball scores to two columns of bowling scores. On Saturday, a double truck of facing pages offered a localized version of *The News'* entertainment guide. It included local restaurant reviews, a best bet listing of movies, concerts, and plays, and a schedule of events ranging from early morning mall walks to quilt shows at the science museum.

Two years later, *The News* launched a similar one-day-a-week section for the Park Cities. Initially, it, too, generated a huge amount of advertising. Given the wealth in the area, every car dealer within fifty miles bought an ad. Eventually, however, the section proved less successful, as advertiser loyalty to two weekly papers in the neighborhood remained strong.

The News has continued to publish both Plano and Park Cities sections, although the Park Cities section is only marginally profitable, and neither of the sections has helped to build much circulation. Most households in these neighborhoods were already subscribing to *The News* before the zoned sections were launched. A characteristic of the Osborne era, however, has been consistency; you don't give people something one day, then take it away the next. "If you do, they won't trust you anymore," he says.

Nonetheless, failure of the Park Cities edition to generate much advertising made *The News* cautious. When community leaders from Arlington, Lewisville/Denton, and Garland/Mesquite later came asking for the same type of specialized coverage, *The News* added localized pages to its metropolitan section instead.

Today the lead story in the Park Cities edition is about Presbyterians at odds with other Presbyterians. A photograph shows liberal dissidents conducting an adult Sunday school class in a neighborhood cafe until another meeting place is ready.

At eleven, editors meet in their small conference room for a presentation of "State of Neglect," a word and photo essay on the Texas environment two years in the making. It will be the year's lead entry for a Pulitzer in the prestigious community service category.

The photographs of an El Paso cemetery covered in lead dust, of pollution at the mouth of the Houston ship channel, and of abandoned, water-filled gravel pits south of Dallas are stronger than the words. A double truck (two facing pages) map depicts the state's trouble spots and can be hung as a poster. Photographer David Leeson makes the presentation.

In the discussion that follows, Leeson and Randy Loftis, the reporter on the project, answer questions. Wilk asks if there are enough wildlife photos to carry the theme of disappearing species. Mong asks for a graph showing not just what the legislature has done, but what it has failed to do; another to show what has been irretrievably lost, next to what can still be saved. Photo editor Davidson and art director Ed Kohorst say they had recommended that the project be published as a self-contained section so more graphics and color could be used, but they have been overruled. Osborne has decided the project will be published as a series, Sunday through Tuesday, to enhance the Monday and Tuesday papers when too few ads run.

Later, however, Osborne changes his mind. He is pleased that the project is "not all advocacy with focus only on the bad guys." He likes that it is "strong on specifics and has something for everybody: details on what the state legislature had accomplished as well as suggestions as to what the average citizen can do." Most of all he likes the seamless blend of words, photographs, and graphics. "They tell the story in such a way that as you move through the text, you experience what is being shown. It's not what everybody likes to hear, but on projects like this, it's often the photographs and graphics that carry the story."

"State of Neglect" was published as a stand alone section on Sunday two weeks later. Six thousand extra copies were given out to school children.

By 1991, *The News* had won a number of journalism's top prizes (three Pulitzers, six Pulitzer runner-ups, a George Polk, a Heywood

The 1986
PULITZER PRIZE
for National Reporting
has been awarded to
Craig Flournoy and George Rodrigue of
The Dallas Morning News
for their series
"Separate and Unequal:
Subsidized Housing in America"

Craig Flournoy, Reporter   George Rodrigue, Reporter   Howard Swindle, Project Editor

At The Dallas Morning News, our primary mission is
to provide our readers with a newspaper of distinction every day.
It is deeply gratifying when our colleagues
recognize our work as the best in the nation
by honoring us with journalism's most prestigious award.

The Dallas Morning News

The 1989
PULITZER PRIZE
for Explanatory Journalism
has been awarded to
David Hanners, William Snyder
and Karen Blessen of
The Dallas Morning News
for their special section
"Anatomy of an Air Crash:
The Final Flight of 50 Sierra Kilo"

| David Hanners, | William Snyder, | Karen Blessen, | Howard Swindle, |
| Reporter | Photographer | Artist | Assistant Managing Editor, Projects |

At The Dallas Morning News, our primary
mission is to provide readers with a newspaper of distinction
every day. It is deeply gratifying when our peers recognize our
work as the best in the nation by honoring us with
journalism's most prestigious award.

The Dallas Morning News

THE 1991

PULITZER PRIZE

FOR FEATURE PHOTOGRAPHY

HAS BEEN AWARDED TO WILLIAM SNYDER OF

THE DALLAS MORNING NEWS FOR HIS WORK ON

THE PLIGHT OF ROMANIA'S ORPHANED CHILDREN.

WILLIAM SNYDER
PHOTOGRAPHER

JOHN DAVIDSON
DIRECTOR OF PHOTOGRAPHY

AT THE DALLAS MORNING NEWS, OUR PRIMARY MISSION IS TO PROVIDE

READERS WITH A NEWSPAPER OF DISTINCTION EVERY DAY. IT IS DEEPLY

GRATIFYING WHEN OUR PEERS RECOGNIZE OUR WORK AS THE BEST IN THE

NATION BY HONORING US WITH JOURNALISM'S MOST PRESTIGIOUS AWARD.

The Dallas Morning News

The 1992
PULITZER PRIZE
for Investigative Reporting
has been awarded to
Lorraine Adams and Dan Malone
of The Dallas Morning News
for their special series
"Abuse of Authority: When
Citizens Complain About Police"

Dan Malone	Lorraine Adams	Howard Swindle
Reporter	*Reporter*	*Assistant Managing Editor, Projects Editor*

At The Dallas Morning News, our primary mission is to provide readers with a newspaper of distinction every day. It is deeply gratifying when our peers recognize our work as the best in the nation by honoring us with journalism's most prestigious award.

The Dallas Morning News

Previous Pulitzer Prizes Awarded: 1986, National Reporting; 1989, Explanatory Journalism; 1991, Feature Photography.

The 1993
PULITZER PRIZE
for Spot News Photography
has been awarded to
Ken Geiger and William Snyder
of The Dallas Morning News
for their series of photographs
of the 1992 Summer Olympics

photo by William Snyder

photo by Ken Geiger

Ken Geiger
Photographer

William Snyder
Photographer

John Davidson
Assistant Managing Editor/Visuals

At *The Dallas Morning News*, our primary mission is to provide readers with a newspaper of distinction every day. It is deeply gratifying when our peers recognize our work as the best in the nation by honoring us with journalism's most prestigious award.

The Dallas Morning News

Previous Pulitzer Prizes Awarded:
1992, Investigative Reporting; 1991, Feature Photography; 1989, Explanatory Journalism; 1986, National Reporting

The 1994
PULITZER PRIZE
for International Reporting
has been awarded to
The Dallas Morning News
for the series
"Violence Against Women:
A Question of Human Rights"

WRITERS

Toni Y. Joseph   Gregory Katz   Melanie Lewis   Victoria Loe   Pam Maples   David L. Marcus   Gayle Reaves   Anne Reifenberg   George Rodrigue

PHOTOGRAPHERS

Paula Nelson   Karen Stallwood   Beatriz Terrazas   Judy Walgren   Cindy Yamanaka

GRAPHICS   EDITORS

Don Huff   Marco A. Ruiz   Kathleen Vincent   John Davidson   Patricia Gaston   Jim Landers

At *The Dallas Morning News*, our primary mission is to provide
readers with a newspaper of distinction every day. It is deeply gratifying
when our peers recognize our work as the best in the nation by
honoring us with journalism's most prestigious award.

The Dallas Morning News

Previous Pulitzer Prizes Awarded:
1993, Spot News Photography; 1992, Investigative Reporting; 1991, Feature Photography; 1989, Explanatory Journalism; 1986, National Reporting

Broun, a Livingston, and a Robert F. Kennedy award). But I hadn't heard much talk about prize winning.

"Whenever we discuss doing a project we have a list of questions we ask," said Osborne, since 1986 a member of the Pulitzer Prize board (in 1995, he would become its chairman). "And I can assure you that none of them is whether it has a chance to win a prize or not. I'm not convinced that prizes attract readers, and what I am concerned about is attracting readers. If our stories attract readers and then win a prize, so much the better."

As a way of discouraging staffers from thinking beyond Dallas, and of keeping egos in check, quarterly in-house contests are held. Judged by a rotating group of reporters and editors, they offer a $100 prize for spot news, feature news, headline writing, page layout, page design, graphics and illustrations, photography, and for a story of less than 600 words. To encourage tighter writing, the prize for the shorter story pays double.

Projects editor Swindle said over half the ideas for investigative or enterprise projects originate with a reporter. And since *The News* doesn't have a star system, it can be a relative newcomer who gets the nod. "Reporters who do good project work tend to be idealistic, since idealism translates into commitment. Usually, these are people who battle their editors over any minor, seemingly insignificant, changes in their copy. For this translates into pride. And often they are people with a need – whether they are aware of it or not – to take their careers to a higher level."

The newsroom's apparent lack of interest in winning prizes might also be attributed to its awareness of the fact that though the *Times Herald* had won more prizes, it was losing the war. Illustrative of *The News'* split personality had been its experience in winning Pulitzers.

Of its three winners so far, two – a series on racial discrimination in public housing, and the anatomy of a plane crash – started as spot stories that grew into something bigger. The third, for feature photography, was a project that would not have been launched had the photographer not been willing to use vacation time.

In April, 1991, William Snyder won the Pulitzer prize for feature photography for a project that photo editor John Davidson neither sponsored, nor initially approved. Snyder, who previously had shared a Pulitzer for "Anatomy of a Plane Crash," proposed a trip to Romania to visit the so-called "homes for the irrecoverables." There, a thousand children infected with the AIDS virus were housed. In a campaign to increase his country's population, President Nicolae Ceausescu had banned contraceptives and most abortions. Dirty needles and tainted blood transfusions were believed responsible for spread of the disease.

Snyder asked Davidson for time to pursue the project, and Davidson said no. The photo department was understaffed and Snyder was needed at home. Snyder persisted, asking if he could use his vacation time, and, if so, would Davidson at least provide film. Davidson finally agreed, and Snyder paid for his travel expenses with freelance money. But because Dallas was still in a recession in 1990, and news space was tight, most of Snyder's prize-winning photographs ran only in the limited Sunday bulldog edition.

Wednesday is when the Food and Fashion ! Dallas sections appear, and both have been losing advertising. The approach of targeting food and fashion sections solely at women in single wage-earner families is out of touch with the times. Advertisers have been abandoning sections in the middle of the paper for positions closer to the front, where they feel stories have higher readership. Editors were revamping both sections.

Today's Fashion ! Dallas features runway coverage of the annual show in Milan (next week it will be Paris and the week after that New York). *The News* has sent a writer and portrait photographer to cover the event, and today's coverage is broader and less upscale than previously. In addition to the fifty-eight photographs (thirty-two of them in color), there are stories about celebrities, people watching, and the bargains to be had.

Likewise, the food section is changing. Today, it features quick and easy recipes that are low in calories and fat, along with a nutrition story. Until recently, the emphasis had been on attractive packaging, "on how pretty we could make the section look," said Mark Weinberg.

"We want to be more useful now." Yet when retail advertising director Jerry Coley looks to see if today the two sections have gained back any lost advertisers, he shakes his head and says, alas no.

Despite improvements in Fashion ! Dallas, many of the upscale boutiques that had advertised there have gone out of business. And despite improvements in the food section, most supermarkets now prefer to place their ads in the A section or in stand alone ("we prints") advertising sections.

Advertisers know "Burl puts his best stories in the A section," says Coley. "Consequently, they see it as the most compelling part of the paper. And 'we prints' are easy to handle. Shoppers carry them into the store with them."

In 1984, *The News* had tried to force supermarkets to advertise in the food section by refusing them space in the "A" section. The *Herald* followed suit, but soon caved in to pressure from its advertisers. Since *The News* couldn't afford to be the only paper with a such a restrictive policy, its attempt failed.

Like most of the country, Dallas experienced a retailing revolution in the late 1980s. Familiar stores were bought by larger companies and given new names. Bloomingdales came and went, Sanger Harris was taken over by Foley's, and many upscale boutiques vanished altogether. Mail order houses flooded the market, and new stores came in – Wal-Mart, Hypermart, Sam's Club, and Food Lion, among others. The new stores elected not to advertise in newspapers as much or, in a few cases, scarcely at all. Most put less emphasis on special sales advertising, and even Sears adopted an everyday low pricing philosophy. Advertisers became increasingly tough-minded, insisting on seeing better results from their ads. Because *The News* kept growing in circulation, and because its readers had higher incomes and more education, these factors, too, played a role in the *Herald's* demise.

Wednesday is also the day when advertising's Don Balser, in charge of new business development, meets with his sales staff. Total market coverage (TMC) falls under new business development, and for the last three years TMC has led all advertising gains.

TMC is a program whereby a department store, supermarket, or restaurant chain can buy one or more zip codes in the neighborhood of its store or stores. *The News* then guarantees saturation coverage of the advertiser's message there. Delivery is to the paper's subscribers through its circulation department, and to non-subscribers by mail. The more subscribers the newspaper has in a given neighborhood, the more cost effective the program is.

As with zoning, *The News* was slow to launch TMC. Here, too, the *Times Herald* had pioneered and failed. But when in 1987, J. C. Penney moved its headquarters to the area, the timing was right. Once Penney showed an interest, Balser and his people got other advertisers to join in, and the program hasn't stopped growing since. Balser attributes TMC's success to the reliability of *The News'* delivery system, to the fact that the paper didn't go to the trouble (and expense) of adding editorial content to the package (instead creating a V-shaped envelope into which pre-prints can be stuffed), and to management's decision to give the staff a generous incentive package. As postal rates have gone up, TMC has cut into direct mail's share of the market.

At the 2:30 news conference, the hot topic is word that a verdict has been reached in the "Danny" Faulkner savings and loan trail. A jury in Midland, Texas, convicted Faulkner and three others of stealing $135 million in a convoluted scheme of land deals that took place in the early 1980s. The verdict ends the longest S & L trial in Texas history and, though belated, shows that bank fraud will not be tolerated.

What gives the event special significance, and contributes to excitement at the news meeting, is the role *The News* played first in uncovering, and then in staying with the story. Investigative reporter Alan Pusey was given the assignment and remained on the case for months, and then years, before seeing his efforts vindicated. By making coverage of savings and loan fraud a priority, *The News* was able to exorcise the ghost of a previous embarrassment – the so-called Golz affair.

Earl Golz was a thirteen-year veteran at *The News* when on July 8, 1982, he wrote a story saying the Abilene National Bank of Abilene, Texas, had a serious loan problem and could soon go under. The story

Front page of the first issue of *The Dallas Morning News.*
Courtesy A. H. Belo Archives.

Commerce Street entrance of the original building of *The Dallas Morning News*. Courtesy A. H. Belo Archives.

Lamar Street entrance of the original building of *The Dallas Morning News*. Courtesy A. H. Belo Archives.

Colonel Alfred H. Belo of *The Dallas Morning News*, 1865–1901.
Courtesy A. H. Belo Archives.

G. B. Dealey, founder and guiding spirit of
The Morning News during the first part of its life.
Courtesy A. H. Belo Corporation Archives.

The Dallas Morning News classified advertising department, April 27, 1925.
Courtesy A. H. Belo Archives.

The Dallas Morning News' "Universal Men" in the 1940s.
Foreground, left to right: Aaron Griffing and J. S. French.
Back, left to right: in the far background is Eli Zeitman, copyboy;
Don MacIver, Robert Lunsford, A. L. (Coke) Wimmer,
David Botter and Elmer G. Luter.
Courtesy A. H. Belo Archives.

Left to right: G. B. Dealey, J. F. Lubben, E. M. (Ted) Dealey,
J. M. Moroney, Leven Deputy, John E. King, J. Q. Dealey, E. B. Doran.
Courtesy A. H. Belo Archives.

The Dallas Morning News building
on Young Street at Houston Street, 1949 to present.
Courtesy A. H. Belo Archives.

ran on page one and triggered an immediate and impassioned response from the bank's chairman. He said the story was totally wrong, and he threatened to bring a $190 million libel suit against the newspaper. Five days later *The News* ran a story on its business front in which the bank chairman was given an opportunity to tell his side of the story. The bank then ran ads in the *Wall Street Journal, Dallas Times Herald, Fort Worth Star-Telegram,* and *Abilene Reporter-News* in further attempts to discredit the report. On July 15, *The New York Times* reported that substantial amounts had been withdrawn from Abilene National in the wake of *The Morning News'* story. *The Times* added the bank had suffered heavy losses on loans for oil and gas ventures, but said Ralph Langer had refused to comment when asked if Golz's report was accurate. Next, *Newsweek* ran an article questioning the accuracy of Golz's story.

Langer then asked Golz and his editor, Wayne Epperson, to resign, Epperson for failing to police Golz properly, Golz for screwing up. Golz added fifteen to twenty inches to his story after it was approved by a senior editor, and Epperson allowed the additions, Langer has said recently. The story was turned in on deadline without the business editor being able to check it for accuracy, as was policy Epperson resigned, and when Golz refused to resign, he was fired.

On August 6, federal bank regulators declared Abilene National to be in imminent danger of failure and forced the bank to close. Subsequent stories by the Associated Press, and in *The New York Times* and *The Washington Post,* reported that Abilene National's loan portfolio was in such bad shape that the bank would have failed even if *The News'* story had not caused a run on its deposits.

The lesson was that if *The News* was to deviate from its policy of positivism towards Texas business institutions, it had better get *all* its facts straight. Although Golz's conclusions were accurate, his story had been flawed in many of its particulars. The incident, which occurred early in Langer's career, convinced him of the need to set up the intricate system of checks and balances that remain in effect today.

This practice of acknowledging past mistakes as a way of preventing their reoccurrence has become something of a fetish at *The News.*

"If you fail to acknowledge the past, you are ill-equipped to see the future very clearly," Robert Decherd has said.

In 1983 (and again in 1988) *The News* published a special section on the anniversary of the death of John F. Kennedy in which Dallas readers were reminded about the full-page ad attacking Kennedy *The News* allowed to run the morning of the day the President was shot.

"Three members of the local John Birch Society wrote that ad," Craig Flournoy reported. "It was paid for by three wealthy Dallas businessmen: oilman Nelson Bunker Hunt, investor H. R. 'Bum' Bright, and insurance executive Edgar Crissey. Bright, whose business interests now include banking and majority interest in the Dallas Cowboys football team, said he had no regrets. 'There was a guy putting the thing together and he came to see me and I gave him some money,' Bright recalled. 'I think I knew the tenor of it [the ad]. I contributed to conservative and right-wing causes, always have and still do.'"

Reporters Steve Blow and Sam Attlesey then wrote that *The News'* editorial page in those years was unswervingly conservative and often acerbic. "Columnists referred to the New Deal as the 'Queer Deal,' to the American Civil Liberties Union as the 'American Swivel Liberties Union,' and to the U.S. Supreme Court as the 'Judicial Kremlin.'"

In a separate piece, Stanley Marcus, chairman emeritus of Neiman Marcus who now writes a weekly column in *The News*, wrote:

"There was a spirit of hate in Dallas then – in the strong Republican districts in North Dallas where people believed they had the only true and revealed truth and could not conceive of any pluralism in society. They were abetted by this newspaper. The Dallas *News* was the one instrument that could have refuted that point of view, but it didn't. It just aided and abetted it."

In a final essay, Blackie Sherrod wrote:

"To Dallas old-timers, the tragedy has become like a birthmark on your child's face. The blemish is there but you have become accustomed to it so that it is no longer a constant heartache. Not until a stranger remarks about it, that is, not until you drive past the old School Book Depository and see tourists at the sixth floor window and unstrapping their Kodaks. And you still feel, however faintly, that stir of resentment and you realize that that day and its shadow will never be erased from memory."

Only by failing to mention that the shooting occurred as the President's limousine passed Dealey Plaza (named after G. B.), did *The News* appear to pull any punches.

In April, 1991, Robert Decherd and Burl Osborne stood in a receiving line next to Caroline and Ethel Kennedy at the Kennedy library in Boston. The occasion was the final reception at the American Society of Newspaper Editors' convention that year. At Osborne's request, John Seigenthaler, who had been Robert Kennedy's administrative assistant (and later publisher of the *Nashville Tennessean*), invited members of the Kennedy family to attend. Seigenthaler is a friend and admirer of Osborne's. "Only a tiny handful of editors have ever transformed a newspaper the way Burl has *The Morning News*," he said.

Late Wednesday afternoon, a wire story came in saying the Drug Enforcement Administration had investigated and found groundless accusations that Vice President Dan Quayle had used cocaine and Quaaludes. These same accusations were about to be resurrected by Garry Trudeau in his comic strip "Doonesbury." *The News* runs "Doonesbury" on its Op Ed page, and since acquiring the strip from the *Times Herald* in 1989, had never censored it.

Langer, who has responsibility for comic strips, and Rena Pederson, who oversees the editorial pages, meet to decide what to do. They agree that the strip should run unchanged, but with an editor's note saying DEA officials had investigated the charges against Mr. Quayle and found them to be groundless.

Twenty-two newspapers throughout the country refused to run the Quayle series, and three others canceled the strip because of Trudeau's attack.

Thursday, November 7

Leading Thursday's paper is a six column headline that reads "Faulkner, 3 others guilty in I-30 case." Beneath the headline are two stories, one describing the verdict, and the other giving background and context. The stories jump to a full page inside where they are accompanied by a graph showing in an easy-to-grasp way just how the condominium scam worked. Prosecutors had feared that murky details of the fraud would be so complex no jury could understand them.

Below the Faulkner stories on page one are two stories out of Washington that underscore President Bush's late start in dealing with the economy. In the center of the page is a 7 by 10 inch color photograph of mayor-elect Bartlett relaxing in his North Dallas home, as his father looks on in approval. David Jackson's story says Bartlett intends to bring major league horse-racing to Dallas, keep Mobil Oil from abandoning downtown, and ensure that police do a better job in combating violent crime. A facts box refers to ten additional election stories inside.

In these stories, as well, the approach is to look forward. One headline reads "Hispanic vote a big factor in Bartlett's win," another says new council members foresee harmony. Candidates facing run-offs say their biggest challenge will be to get the voters to the polls. Except to mention that there was an unexpectedly large turnout of voters, no attempt is made to analyze why a white and a white-supported black candidate are leading in two of the five majority black council districts.

In his one local cartoon of the week, Bill DeOre shows two businessmen standing in an empty field looking at an oversized woman's shoe. The shoe, labeled Dallas, is coming apart at the seams. "Well, Steve," the older man says, "you've got some mighty big shoes to fill."

The Steve is mayor-elect Steve Bartlett, and the reference is to the administration of outgoing mayor, Annette Strauss, who happens to be the mother-in-law of Jeremy Halbreich, *The News*' president and general manager. The image-conscious *News*, a reflection of image conscious Dallas, has been critical of Strauss for lack of decisiveness and failure to maintain order and decorum in City Council chambers. Against the unanimous recommendation of Rena Pederson's editorial board, *The News* failed to endorse Strauss when she ran for mayor.

DeOre, a Dallas native and twenty-two-year veteran at *The News*, seldom publishes more than one local cartoon a week. Like most cartoonists at newspapers the size of *The Morning News*, he is a member of the Universal Press Syndicate. As such, he is obliged to put four national or international cartoons on the UPS wire each week. Cartoons from other cartoonists in the syndicate also regularly run in *The News*.

Osborne has no problem with this de-emphasis on local cartooning. He admits to being uncomfortable with "messages that cut or bite or hurt someone. When we're trying to be reflective of the total community, we don't contribute anything by screaming and shouting. It's hard to persuade someone who is thoroughly pissed off at you."

Osborne would prefer that DeOre be less visceral, "be more like an editorial writer with a different set of tools," but hasn't made an issue of it. Pederson, more protective, said she sees DeOre as "a peacock, not as a chicken who lays a labeled egg." She allows him more freedom than she does her editorial writers, and reins him in only when he, "like most cartoonists," gets bawdy. "He has this thing about, if you'll pardon the impression, butt cracks." Pederson and DeOre agree that the most sensitive areas are cartoons depicting African-Americans and Arabs. Puffy lips, popping eyes, and burnooses are all taboo.

In "Sports Day," Cowboys' coach Jimmy Johnson is saying in his weekly column that Sunday's game with the Oilers "could present the most difficult challenge we've faced since I've been a part of the team."

Today's lead obituary is about a local judge who suffered health problems after being exposed to Agent Orange. "He was killed twenty years ago," says his wife Peggy. "It just took him twenty-three years to die."

Obituaries are among the best-read parts of the paper, and *The News* has them anchored at the back of its metropolitan section. Usually they are written by a veteran reporter who has knowledge of the people involved. People who have touched a lot of lives – teachers, preachers, and celebrities – are awarded a story rather than a death notice. Former newspaper employees also rate a story, as does anyone recommended by Robert Decherd, Joe Dealey, or former editor, Tom Simmons.

At 9:30, writing coach Paula LaRocque arrives to distribute F.Y.I., her occasional newsletter that critiques stories and headlines. A former journalist and college professor, LaRocque has been at the paper since 1981. She became Ralph Langer's first hire after Osborne said he was dismayed at the unevenness and inconsistency he found in reporting styles. LaRocque's mandate is to improve writing skills and discourage reporting that slides over into opinion or advocacy. *The News* uses the AP stylebook, which she helped localize and expand.

Her dictums include: A sentence with more than twenty-three words is usually too long; if you're doing a story with numbers or statistics, ask for a graphic or a bar chart; and if you can't explain something simply (credit crunch, for example), you shouldn't be writing about it. She says that instead of saying someone lives in a posh or pricey house or in an exclusive neighborhood, you should write he or she lives in a $300,000 home, and let the reader decide. She rails against the elevated tone big stories often generate, against quotes that sound too formal, and against business and political writers who write for their sources or other writers.

She tells reporters to expunge from their copy clichés like window of opportunity, critical mass, political football, déjà vu, firestorm of criticism, cautious optimism, litmus test, and laundry list – and judgmental verbs such as concede, contend and vow. She warns against headlines that present stereotypes, or go for the sensational: "AA member charged in traffic deaths," "High school dropout held in sexual abuse case," "Ex-Marine goes on shooting spree," and "Baptist slays family, self." And she has set up a mentoring program. Veteran reporters and columnists work with reporters who want – or need – to expand their repertoire. Blackie Sherrod has been showing entertainment writer Shermakaye Bass how to write in the first person without saying "I" or "me," for example.

Some women reporters complain that LaRocque's insistence on courtesy titles make their stories sound Victorian. Sports writers say she has little appreciation for the pressures of writing under a tight deadline. But even her detractors say she makes them think.

Courtesy titles are used in all except sports stories, and even in sports if the story starts on page one. Courtesy titles are used for convicted felons, including serial killers (Mr. Manson, for example), although not for people like Hitler or Madonna. Men and women are addressed as Mr., Ms., Miss, or Mrs., or, if they prefer, given an appropriate professional title such as Dr., detective, or staff sergeant. LaRocque says that for years she believed the only route to equality was to eliminate courtesy titles altogether. Her thinking changed when she realized there are male and female titles – Mr. and Ms. – that are essentially equal and make no reference to marital status.

Until a few years ago, she spent most of her time in Dallas, but now she is often traveling. She conducts workshops at the American Press

Institute, at the Washington Bureau of the Associated Press, and at newspapers that don't belong to chains.

In today's F.Y.I., she praises metro reporter Anne Belli for a sentence pruned of all but the essentials ("the drug dealer was shot three times, run over by a car, and left in a puddle of water"); editor Mike Finn for the headline "Room for improvement; La Quinta receives a mixed report card as motel chain cuts back," and Barry Horn for this lead:

"They are a couple of middle-aged guys who blew into town a couple of months apart a couple of years ago.

"One arrived on a white horse, the other on a broom. Nothing in our world of sports has been the same since.

"You loved Nolan Ryan from the start. Jerry Jones, it took some time getting used to."

At eleven, editors meet for their ritual post mortem on the election coverage. This is Stu Wilk's meeting and attending are managing editor Mong, metro editor Bailon, two former metro political reporters, Kevin Merida and Mark Edgar, assistant news editor Rick Barrick, and the current metro political editor, Dave Flick. Flick, who appears not to have much supervision or encouragement to take risks, wants to know "how can we do better next time?"

He gets an earful. Wilk says "We were too cautious. In most stories, reporters failed to call the election even after the results were obvious." Mong notes that in last year's state-wide election, the Austin bureau had a system which enabled them to anticipate the unexpected and respond. (The Austin bureau also has a sophisticated computer system which allows it to analyze campaign funding.)

Kevin Merida, now in charge of national and international reporting, says the coverage was lacking in mood and context, too narrowly specific. "Why wasn't there more analysis? We knew the bellwether precincts, didn't we? Analysis is what we can do better than television. With analysis, we could have debunked Bartlett's claim that he won with strong minority support."

Metro editor Bailon defends his decision to bury Lawrence Young's analysis story, saying he needed room nearer the front for his story about unexpectedly large voter turnout. Others say too many statistics gave the front page a boring black and gray look. No one suggests any follow-up stories. Ralph Langer had already expressed himself satisfied with the coverage.

"1A accomplished our goal of giving a roundup of major stories in graphic form," he wrote in a memo. "Pages were well designed and packaged with a good mix of photos. . . . Good choice of expressions on photos from the Pa. race. Wofford looks pleased, Thornburgh vexed. . . . We need to be careful in referring to council districts though. We should not be calling them 'safe black (or Hispanic) seats or districts.' Correct reference is 'predominantly black (or Hispanic) district.' Safe implies that a person of a different race could not win an election there."

Osborne, on his return from the East Coast, agreed. He said because of the many new and unknown council candidates, and the long and bitter controversy over redistricting, the newsroom had been wise to tread lightly. They hadn't done a computer analysis of campaign contributions, the way the Austin bureau does, because it's been harder to gain access to data bases in Dallas. And yes, reporters assigned to the local political beats were relative newcomers, but in times of turmoil, you don't want people with a fixed mind set covering sensitive issues. Osborne gave metro editor Gilbert Bailon (a month later promoted to assistant managing editor) credit for steering a balanced and prudent course. "At least we avoided a 'Joe Bob' incident," Osborne said.

The "Joe Bob" incident was an affair that helped seal the fate of the *Dallas Times Herald*. Later, it came to be the subject of an article spoofing Dallas by Calvin Trillin in *The New Yorker*.

"Joe Bob goes to the drive-in" was a column written by John Bloom. Intended as a harmless satire on the workings of the redneck mind, it had already drawn protests from women (who didn't like being called bimbos), gays (offended by the San Francisco jokes), Hispanics (who didn't appreciate being called "Meskins"), and Baptists (who objected to all the sex and violence).

No protest matched in intensity, however, the demonstration that followed the appearance on April 12, 1985, of a column titled "We are the weird" (a satire on the We are the World campaign). "There are Negroes dying; and it's time we make 'em eat," Bloom wrote. "We are the weird; we are the starvin,' we are the scum of the filthy earth."

Led by County Commissioner John Wiley Price, three hundred African-Americans marched on the *Times Herald*. They demanded an apology, cancellation of the column, and the hiring of twelve black journalists, two in high places. Over the objections of at least one senior editor, Times Mirror and the *Herald's* publisher quickly capitulated, the column was killed, and Bloom resigned in protest. Bloom's column now runs in the *Dallas Observer*, an alternative weekly.

At noon Thursday, sports editor Dave Smith was eating lunch with Tom Grieve, general manager of the Texas Rangers. The lunch had been Smith's idea, triggered by criticism of two of his writers on Norm Hitzges' KLIF talk show. Hitzges had spent an hour interviewing Rangers' coach Bobby Valentine at the coach's bar and grill in Arlington.

"How does it feel to manage a team for seven years and never be in contention?" Hitzges asked. "Do you feel as if you are about to lose your job?"

Valentine said the Rangers had had a winning record the last three seasons.

"What grade would you give yourself?"

"A passing grade. Neither an A nor a C."

"How do you react to the beating you are taking in the press? To a *Morning News* columnist calling for your dismissal?"

(The week before Randy Galloway had written that Valentine should be fired. He said the Rangers had the best offense and finest young talent in baseball and that no manager had ever been with a team this long without winning something.)

"You have to consider the source," Valentine said. "*The Morning News* doesn't think I help them sell newspapers. I'd been warned last Spring that they were out to get me."

"Have you been having trouble with their beat writer, Gerry Fraley?"

"Yes, I have," said Valentine. "Fraley and I don't have the professional relationship you'd expect, or hope for, with someone you have to work with every day. Fraley thinks I favor writers from the other papers. Which, of course, isn't true."

Smith, who listens to Hitzges' talk show on his way to work every morning, was upset. He called KLIF and asked for a tape of the show. He said he thought it hypocritical for Hitzges to be promoting Valentine's bar and grill while pretending to be neutral. He asked to appear on Hitzges' show himself, but by the time he did, he had cooled off. Rather than prolong the controversy on the air, he elected to meet with Valentine's boss Tom Grieve instead.

Yes, *The News* had been tough on Valentine, but in Smith's view, the coach deserved it. Valentine was too emotional, too up and down, not the steadying influence his young ballplayers needed. The Rangers had been in first place at the All-Star break, but by Labor Day they had dropped out of contention.

Galloway had also hammered George W. Bush, the Ranger's managing partner (and son of President Bush) in a column. Smith had agreed with Randy then, too. But in September, Fraley wrote a story in which he asked whether the Rangers were a success because of a third consecutive season with record attendance, or a third consecutive failure because they were going to finish ten games behind the division champions again. Fraley wrote that, like owners of the Baltimore Orioles, Bush and his people cared only about making a profit.

Smith said he felt nothing should be done to rein in Galloway. Randy was a columnist and his job was to write opinion. Galloway had been covering the Rangers since 1966, and his talk show on WBAP had more listeners than did Hitzges' on KLIF. Nor did Smith want to inhibit Fraley. He often called Fraley the best beat writer in baseball.

Because of the Texas heat, the Rangers play nearly all their games at night, and Fraley was always at the ballpark by three or four in the afternoon. He talked with every player every day and kept a more complete set of statistics than the Rangers did, updating them each night before going to bed. On weekends, Fraley took Spanish lessons so players like Ruben Sierra would level with him. The night Nolan Ryan pitched his seventh no-hitter, Fraley had sensed by the third inning Ryan was untouchable. He picked up the phone and called for help and in its coverage the next day *The News* smothered the competition.

Smith didn't intend to inhibit Fraley, but it was important that the lines of communication stay open. Fraley could be hardheaded and Valentine was extremely sensitive. And so over lunch today Smith was asking Grieve to arrange for Valentine and Fraley to meet and work out their differences. Grieve said he would see what he could do. He said Fraley was so knowledgeable that his questions sometimes sounded like an attack.

At the 2:30 news conference, stories proposed include one from Rome where President Bush had told Europeans the U.S. still has an important role to play in NATO, and another from Washington about abortion rights advocates challenging the Supreme Court to reaffirm Roe vs. Wade. Metro has a report saying Dallas schools have lower test scores and higher dropout rates than other Texas cities. And international editor Landers is again trying to sell a *New York Times* story which his assistant, Patricia Gaston is pushing. The story claims that fifty to a hundred million Asian women are missing, having been killed at birth, or allowed to die as a result of cultural misogyny. Landers isn't having much luck. Neither the *Times* nor the *Wall Street Journal* gave the story prominent play. (Ironically, three years later, *The News* will win a Pulitzer for a series about violence against women that incorporates some of this same information.)

It looks like another slow news day until just before four, when a bulletin comes in saying Magic Johnson has scheduled a five o'clock press conference. The word is that he will announce he has contracted the AIDS virus. Among senior editors, the rumor of Johnson's affliction had been circulating for days. Veteran columnist Blackie Sherrod heard it first, then NBA beat writer David Moore. They informed Dave Smith, who told Ralph Langer, but scarcely anyone else knew.

Seldom do all senior editors and all department heads attend the 4:30 news meeting, but today they do. All twenty chairs are filled and people are standing along the walls. Evans asks sports to lead off first and Smith tells some of what he knows. He doesn't mention the rumors about bisexuality or his columnists' suspicion that Johnson contracted the disease from a man.

"A senior editor mentions a rumor and people jump on it as fact," Smith would say later. "Best not to bring it up. Best not to have people running around speculating. Especially not a rumor of this magnitude."

"We try never to say 'we can't verify this, but the word is going around . . .'" Langer explained. "If we hear the mayor is sleeping with a restaurant owner to whom he gives licensing favors, that's something we would look into. But if he is sleeping with someone in his social circle, probably not."

Bob Mong quickly makes a list of tentative story assignments, seventeen in all. *The News* prides itself on its ability to surround a big, fast-breaking story. When something important happens, Osborne's goal is to give tomorrow's readers as much information as they can find later in a magazine like *Time* or *Newsweek*. He discourages second and third day repetition or rehash, on grounds that they lack freshness. After Bob Mong beat out Dave Smith for the managing editor's job, the defining moment is said to have been Mong's performance in 1985 when he mobilized the newsroom to cover the worst air crash in Texas history. Years earlier, when John Hinkley tried to kill President Reagan, Burl Osborne had the newsroom put out its first extra edition ever. "You put out an extra," he said, "and you find out who's up to the challenge. What kind of people you want to build upon."

David Moore is assigned the lead Johnson story, plus a sidebar on reaction from Isiah Thomas and Mark Aguirre, two of Johnson's friends. Aguirre, a former star player with the Mavericks, is well known in Dallas. The business desk will poll corporate America to determine how having the AIDS virus may affect Johnson's product endorsements. Sports will have a second story on page one about local playground reaction. Metro will have stories inside on reaction from Dallas' gay community, and on the probable effect on AIDS funding. News art will prepare a graphic on what parents should say to their children, a facts box on Johnson's career, and another on how Johnson got the name Magic. Smith will have Kevin Blackistone do an appreciation of Johnson, the athlete. Smith also will be on the lookout for columns from other NBA cities. Stallings' lead story for Sunday will be about the deeper issues involved.

Smith leaves the meeting and goes back to his windowless office at the other end of the newsroom. He turns on his television set, sits in silence, and soon begins shaking his head. A reporter asks Johnson how he thinks he acquired the virus.

"We'll get into that medically with the doctors," Johnson says.

There is no follow-up. "Johnson has always been a media favorite," Smith says. "Always smiling, always accommodating, always quick with the memorable quote."

Smith adds another item to his list of stories for tomorrow's paper. Barry Horn will critique Johnson's press conference.

Friday, November 8

Two stories about Magic Johnson lead Friday's front page and two more its sports front. Twelve other Johnson stories, columns and briefs appear inside. "NBA now a game without Magic" reads the headline on the sports front. "New York coach Pat Riley choked back tears Thursday as he led everyone at Madison Square Garden in a prayer for his friend," the story begins.

In his critique of the press conference, Barry Horn says the question of how Johnson acquired the AIDS virus will have to be asked "again and again, if necessary. . . . It was Johnson, after all, who said he wanted to be a spokesman against the killer disease. . . . By not pressing for an explanation at his press conference, the news media failed him. . . . Surely, Johnson's anger could not be anymore damaging than the speculation that is sure to follow."

In its advice on what to tell children, *The News* suggests:

"Q. How did Magic Johnson get the disease?

"A. We don't know. It's too late to wonder how he got it. He may have done something without taking proper precautions.

"Q. Will he die?

"A. Everybody is going to die. Anybody could go outside and get hit by a truck and die or have a heart attack and die.

"Q. Is he gay?

"A. You can't determine whether a person is gay or straight by them having HIV. Anybody is at risk if they are having unprotected sex or sharing needles.

"Q. Is Magic Johnson a bad person?

"A. No. Everybody makes mistakes, and sometimes people suffer consequences from their mistakes."

In their placement of stories, editors have taken care not to be provocative or give offense. Horn's critique of the press conference and a pessimistic story about Johnson's future product endorsements don't appear until deep in the sports section.

By mid-morning other Johnson stories are being developed, but by then, more important events are taking place behind the scenes.

Burl Osborne is back in Dallas having cut short his trip to the East Coast. He has been summoned by Belo president Jim Sheehan, who is unhappy with the strategy Langer and Osborne have developed to combat a libel suit.

The suit resulted from a series of stories on illegal drug trafficking which *The News* had published the year before. The sheriff of Starr County, Texas, claims the paper falsely accused him, by both innuendo and direct allegation, of involvement in the trafficking. At issue is whether the anonymity of certain sources the reporters used can still be protected.

The series, titled "Tales of two counties: Texas' little Columbia," was published following a year-long investigation by veteran reporters Gayle Reaves, David Hanners, and David McLemore. The reporters interviewed scores of residents, community leaders, and convicted and suspected drug dealers. They also examined hundreds of court records and police reports. The reporters showed that drug money taints virtually every facet of life along the easternmost stretch of the Texas/Mexico border. And they chronicled the frightening effect that drugs have on the life of ordinary citizens. The series challenged the belief of some that the citizens there wink and nod at the traffic which passes through their homeland.

The sheriff had asked the court to take depositions from people he suspected of having made accusations against him. The reporters feared that several of their informants' lives could be endangered if their names were revealed. Langer's and Osborne's strategy was that only in the event one of these sources admitted to having talked with *The News*, but gave a different and damaging account as to what had been said, would their testimony be challenged at this early stage in the proceedings. If they denied talking with the reporters, they could, if necessary, be challenged later.

Belo president Jim Sheehan disagreed with this strategy. He considered little perjury and big perjury to be the same thing. He feared if Belo didn't challenge on both counts now, the company could find itself in a worse position later on, and was not willing to take that risk. Eight months before, Belo's insurance carrier had forced the company to settle, rather than appeal, a $58 million award against WFAA, its Dallas TV station.

That case had been heard in Waco, Texas, a city close to Dallas. Victor Feazel, then district attorney for McLennan County, had filed the suit claiming to have been defamed by Channel 8's eleven-part series which portrayed him as a lax and corrupt prosecutor. Feazel was indicted on charges of racketeering, bribery, and mail fraud, but later acquitted. And the libel trial didn't take place until five years later. By then, two of the Channel 8 reporter's sources denied statements credited to them.

Although jury awards in libel suits are often reduced or overturned on appeal, Belo had had no choice but to settle. Given the size of the verdict, the insurance carrier gave the company the option of either settling or proceeding without benefit of coverage. Had Belo appealed, the insurance carrier would have had to bear the burden of interest charges pending final settlement.

Consequently, in the South Texas case, Sheehan was taking no chances. He said he was concerned about the public's growing distrust of the media, and about the tendency of local juries to favor hometown Davids over big city Goliaths. By the time Osborne returned to Dallas Friday, Sheehan had developed a new strategy.

Osborne wasn't happy about this turn of events. He thought the series was bulletproof, and that the information contributed by unnamed sources was not vital to its credibility. He thought Sheehan's strategy was based on a lot of "what ifs," rather that on what was *likely* to happen. The stories had been gone over by a lawyer on retainer to the newsroom. Osborne didn't relish the thought of embarrassing his editors or undermining his reporters, but because a part of his job is to act as a buffer between corporate interests and the news department, he didn't object.

He passed the word to Langer, who this same Friday meets with the reporters and their editors. At the meeting, no one except Langer says very much. The atmosphere is somber. Langer tells the reporters to advise their sources that they will have to be identified and can soon be challenged. Depositions are scheduled to be taken early the following week. The reporters again say they fear that lives will be endangered. They say they feel they are being asked to go back on their word. But so far, no one refuses to cooperate.

The newsroom has a policy in a memo signed by Langer, and dating to 1983, stating that no unnamed sources will be used without a supervisory editor being made aware and approving. The approving editor must then notify his or her department head as well as a senior editor. "Unnamed sources must be made to understand that they can ultimately be called upon to identify themselves and testify as to what has been said," the memo reads.

The problem was that the rules had not been enforced. The reporters, if they were aware of the policy, elected to forget. And their editors, knowing how difficult it is for Anglo reporters to get Mexican-Americans in South Texas to talk candidly about sensitive issues, elected to be lenient, as well.

Three days after the session in Langer's offices, when it came time for one of the reporters to give Belo's lawyer the details under which a conversation between reporter and source occurred, the reporter balked. All three reporters then refused to cooperate further, and said they wanted to hire their own lawyer. Confusion reigned.

The next morning, Belo's attorneys persuaded the judge to postpone the hearing at which depositions were to be taken, and another meeting took place between reporters and management. This time, however, the meeting wasn't held in the friendly confines of Langer's office, but across the street in Belo's corporate board room. And although Burl Osborne sat at one end of the table and the three reporters at the other, with editors and lawyers in between, this was clearly Jim Sheehan's meeting. Robert Decherd was out of town, and later said he didn't hear about the meeting until months later.

Sheehan, who spent the first part of the meeting listening, said he had no problem with the three reporters hiring their own attorney. So long as they found someone credible, Belo would pay the bill. What Sheehan wanted to know was did the reporters see themselves as free agents? Did they see *The Morning News* as only a vehicle through which they printed their stories? Just where did their loyalties lie? What did they think should take precedence, the possible loss of a $100 million libel suit, or the protection of a few anonymous sources who, according to the newsroom's own guidelines, should have been told in the first place that they couldn't be protected? Although Sheehan was Osborne's boss, the reporters had never seen him in action before.

The reporters reluctantly agreed to the new strategy; they had no choice. The source in question testified that he had talked to the reporters and had said what they attributed to him. He added, moreover, that the sheriff's people had offered him a bribe if he would change his story. An appeals court later reversed a lower court order saying the reporters must reveal their sources. And Belo eventually agreed to a face-saving settlement under which the company would give $45,000, not to the sheriff, but to help build a youth center in Rio Grande, Texas.

It seemed a happy ending, but the incident left scars. Langer and his editors felt they had been humiliated. Reporters called the affair an "end to innocence." And relations between Osborne and Jim Sheehan would never be the same again.

This same Friday, Langer had another unpleasant duty to perform – postpone again resumption of the "Abuse of Authority" series, which had started its run in March, been abruptly discontinued in April, and was tentatively scheduled to resume on Sunday.

The series was written by Lorraine Adams, a stylish writer and Princeton graduate who had been editor of the school's literary magazine, and Dan Malone, a Dallas native and former investigative reporter for the *Fort Worth Star-Telegram*. Originally, the idea was Adams.' She had previously written a series about Dallas police shootings, and said that while doing it she discovered that people in authority can often lie. Malone joined the project later, in part because editors feared for Adams' safety. "Lorraine is a quick study, bright, tenacious," said projects editor Swindle. "We needed a good ol' boy who could talk trash to the cops. There aren't a lot of good ol' boys at *The Morning News*."

"The Abuse of Authority" series said Texas law enforcement officers were the most frequently investigated group in the nation. A map showed which counties, and which police departments in each county, had the most civil rights investigations pending. The two reporters documented cases in which police officers beat and killed citizens, seemingly without justification, and they showed that these same officers then were often given a judicial benefit of doubt not accorded ordinary citizens. The reporters made extensive use of the Texas Open Records and Federal Freedom of Information Acts to force uncooperative agencies to open their files. The documents revealed a trend of entrepreneurial law enforcement that showed drug busts were being made less because of suspected criminal involvement than on the basis of how much cash and other assets could be seized.

The first story was rushed into print March 17, fourteen days after Rodney King's beating by Los Angeles police officers. Given the timeliness of the subject matter, editors allowed the series to start its run before all stories were written. Five page-one stories ran between March 17 and April 21, each accompanied by an "Abuse of Authority" logo. Headlines read: "Texas leads nation in police abuse," "Despite video of beating, Austin officer keeps job," and "Stun gun victim leaves state: Officer wins job back." The reporters were critical not just of Texas law enforcers, but of the civil rights division of the U.S. Justice Department, which had refused to explain its rationale for not prosecuting many of the cases.

Osborne was out of town when the stories began their run. After he returned, and read them as a group, he took exception to the logo. He thought "Abuse of Authority" was too judgmental. Were the stories to run consecutively, one day after another, there wouldn't be a problem. But since they had been running intermittently – and would continue to run that way – it sounded as if *The Morning News* was saying all Texas police officers abused their authority. Obviously this wasn't so.

Osborne had no problem with the stories' contents, but asked that before the series resumed, the logo be changed. The logo came across as too sweeping. Editors were informed, as were the two reporters.

The reporters were incensed. They wanted to talk with Osborne to appeal his decision on the grounds that any change at this late date could be interpreted as a reflection on their work. Obviously, the publisher could do what he liked, but *The Morning News* had an open door policy, didn't it?

Their editors all urged the reporters to cease and desist. They had worked long enough with Osborne to know he wouldn't change his mind. But Adams, in particular, was insistent. And so Malone crafted a letter which the two reporters signed, then he carried it upstairs.

As it happened, Osborne was standing outside his office door that day. His office has a homey feel. Its windows look out towards the Dallas skyline and the walls are bright with one red and yellow painting and another in blues and purples. But Osborne tries not to spend too much time in his office. Never one to schedule himself too tightly, he likes to stay open to the unexpected. The unexpected is what makes his days interesting, he says. He is known to pace, to wander in and out of other peoples' work spaces, to be constantly on the move. And so Malone was able to deliver his letter in person.

"We understand you feel the logo should be modified," it began. We respect the fact that the decision rests with you.

"We also hope you won't think us disrespectful for expressing our reservations about modifying the logo. We have previously voiced them in person to Ralph Langer, Bill Evans, Bob Mong and Howard Swindle.

"First, pride of authorship isn't at issue here. 'Abuse of Authority' was Howard Swindle's and Bob Mong's creation, not ours.

"The logo, as you are aware, has run on the front page of *The News* five times. The series has been cited by more than two dozen news organizations, including *The New York Times*, *The Washington Post*, the *Chicago Tribune* and ABC News. The reporting has been praised as even-handed and professional from such unlikely sources as John Dunne, chief of the U.S. Justice Department's Civil Rights Division. To our knowledge, no one has complained that the logo is a departure from *The News'* high standards of fairness.

"The logo is the only part of the project common to all the stories. We feel continuity and consistency is important to the perception that *The News* is sticking to the commitment it made to this project two years ago, long before the civil rights issue was thrown into the national spotlight.

"Changing the logo at this time, we fear, will send troubling messages to readers, colleagues, and sources. To readers, it may signal confusion. To colleagues, it may raise questions of conviction and resolve. To sources – citizens and police officers – it may well appear that *The Dallas Morning News* is taking a step backwards and saying, we're not sure about what we have published.

"And on a personal level, which admittedly shouldn't figure prominently in any decision, changing the logo is demoralizing. It's like having the rug pulled from under your feet.

"If we didn't share common concerns about *The News'* well deserved reputation for excellence, such a seemingly minor detail wouldn't be an issue for any of us. And we hope you'll understand our need to express our views before a change is made.

"Thank you for your consideration."

Osborne read the letter. He was not impressed.

Minutes later, he was on the third floor, in Bill Evans' office. Langer, Mong, and Swindle were there, too. Adams and Malone were summoned, ushered in, and told to sit in the two chairs that had been placed in the center of the room. Osborne then subjected Malone to a barrage of questions while Adams sat with her head in her hands.

Did the two reporters think they should also be writing headlines? Osborne wanted to know.

"No," said Malone.

How long had they been working on this series?

"More than two years."

Did they have any idea as to when they would be finished?

"Not exactly."

How many stories did they eventually expect to write?

"Twenty to twenty-four."

"I'm not sure I'd want to read that many stories about the Second Coming," Osborne said.

His decision would stand. The logo would be changed or modified. No further stories would run until all were completed, and had passed muster. Ralph Langer would decide when. Osborne would not look at any of the stories again until they were in the paper.

Word of the confrontation had spread throughout the newsroom. Opinion split between those who thought that the paper's fairness doctrine had been upheld, and those who felt *The News'* open door policy was now a myth. Adams and Malone complained that in the meeting with Osborne their editors had said nothing in their defense. Adams later said, "I know Burl's an astonishing talent. I know he's responsible for turning this paper around. But I felt as if I'd been squished like a bug. Only Howard [Swindle] gave me the emotional support to keep going. These men don't understand you don't get a good performance by threat and intimidation, but by inspiring and encouraging."

On this Friday in November, Langer is almost satisfied that the "Abuse of Authority" series is ready to resume. There isn't much time left. It needs to be published in its entirety by year's end if it is to be submitted for a Pulitzer. Already, its chances of winning have been lessened because the prize is seldom awarded for stories that don't result in corrective action being taken.

Langer is almost satisfied, but then sees that the editors before him have failed to prune all the unnecessary embellishments – an occasional "indeed," and several phrases like "he claimed" or "he contended" instead of the unvarnished "he said."

The series finally resumed nine days later. The logo was changed to read "Abuse of Authority: When Citizens Complain about Police." No significant changes were made to any of the stories, but there was a new, more temperate overview. Among other things, it said:

"Every four days, a person dies at the hands of Texas law enforcement. . . .[But] more than sixty per cent of the deaths occurred in jail. . . . [T]he majority were from natural causes or suicides . . . [and] in many of the confrontations, witnesses corroborated the need for officers' use of lethal force. . . .[N]o criminal action was taken in ninety per cent of the deaths."

Paul Watler, the lawyer on retainer to the newsroom and the one who checked the stories for possible libel, said he had wanted to know very specifically who was being accused of doing something wrong. He wanted to discourage use of the broad brush, the global, and overly inclusive. "You can't anticipate a possible libel suit unless you know who's being accused of what."

Otherwise, Friday turns out to be a normal day.

The House & Garden section had continued to enjoy good advertising support, and today it was easy to understand why. The lead story is about "why fireplaces are better than ever; some don't even need a chimney." A second story titled "Repairs, when little things go wrong" shows homeowners how to get results from their builder's customer service department, and a column offers advice to both organic and traditional gardeners. Editor Bob Bersano's philosophy is that few people are do-it-yourself experts; most are starting from scratch.

Leading the business front is a story by Terry Maxon saying American Airlines expects to post a fourth-quarter loss. It includes an analysis showing why the first and fourth quarters are invariably the weakest for airlines, plus American's complaint that other airlines, particularly bankrupt carriers, are pricing tickets to pay daily expenses rather than meet long term objectives.

American is the Dallas/Ft. Worth area's largest employer, and its CEO, Robert Crandall, one of the region's most powerful and outspoken executives. With real estate still in the doldrums and Dallas in the corporate relocation business, Crandall controls D/FW airport, the area's biggest draw. When American first moved its headquarters to Texas, Crandall was outspokenly critical of newspapers. He is less so now. If his airline has a problem, he knows that *The News*, in writing the story, will put American's difficulties into perspective.

On today's metro front, Ann Belli has a story showing why new court rules make divorces harder to get. Bob Mong sends her a congratulatory note and asks Stu Wilk why her story wasn't pitched for page one.

After Sunday's, Friday's paper is the week's largest, and it is heavy in entertainment news. On the Today section front are three movie reviews, each accompanied by a color photograph. Movies are big in Dallas, and it's an important test market. Stephen Spielberg brought *Close Encounters of the Third Kind*, *Jaws*, and *Hook* here before release to see if they needed further refinements. *The News* has two movie reviewers – Philip Wuntch, who covers the big ticket items, and Russell Smith, who reviews most of the foreign films.

Movie house managers defer to Wuntch. He prides himself on not being cutthroat. He tries to like all the movies he sees, if not in their entirety, at least in part. At previews, he's awarded the best seat in the house. His lead review today is on *Black Robe*, a film whose "startling beauty is balanced by an equally startling savagery." Chief Chomina is "warmhearted without inviting the condescending phrase of folksy. . . . Alden Young's portrayal of the eager Daniel has spontaneity . . . [and] the heroine's appeal is along more elemental lines." Wuntch awarded *Black Robe* three-and-a-half stars. His review appears again in the weekend Guide section, also part of the Friday paper.

The tabloid-size Guide section allots two full pages to listings of forty movies currently showing in the area. Most are accompanied by an abbreviated review, and beside each listing are two or more symbols (a heart for romantic, a teddy bear for children's appeal, clapping hands for a crowd pleaser, etc.) A few R-rated movies are briefly described, but most – *Rapture*, *Prime Target*, and *Drowning by the Numbers* – are merely listed by name.

The Guide section was one of Robert Decherd's first projects (Fashion ! Dallas another). Launched in 1976, Guide built on the reader-service examples of *Philadelphia* and *New York* magazines. The first issue featured "cleaner, brighter graphics and thousands of listings on where to dine, play, and have fun." The format has hardly changed since.

Today's Guide has fifty-two pages and includes one major restaurant review, five smaller restaurant reviews, and six hundred other restaurant listings, all carrying a brief description and, in many cases, a review rating. Restaurants are alphabetized by type (Italian, Tex-Mex, new American casual, eclectic, mall food, etc.), and the reviews are almost always positive in tone. Should a reviewer visit a restaurant and have a bad experience, the restaurant is visited again, and if it is still unsatisfactory, it is usually not reviewed. Sometimes Waltrina Stovall, the lead reviewer, will offer suggestions to restaurant owners as a group: "Tell your diners if the lasagna was made on the premises or at the House of Frozen Foods, . . . no small print on the menus please, . . . no tacky foil on the baked potatoes." Occasionally, metro columnist Bob St. John will pass along advice from waiters and waitresses: "Don't snap your fingers or whistle to get our attention, we're not animals; don't turn us into runners, please bunch your requests; on busy nights, don't wait too long before ordering." And in his society column, Alan Peppard often prints names of the places where sports stars and other celebrities dine. Given so much free publicity, restaurants are not big advertisers.

Guide also includes previews of coming events, and this week these include a Luther Vandross concert at Reunion Arena; a literary festival at SMU; the play *Substance of Fire* at the Dallas Theater Center; Joseph Brenna and Kristin Kunhardt singing folk music at Poor David's Pub; Riders in the Sky at Ft. Worth's Caravan of Dreams; and Patti LaBelle at the Great Hall of the Apparel Mart. There follows a five-page listing of activities ranging from polo lessons to job hunting workshops.

Here, too, readers find the greatest concentration of ads for events for which *The News* acts as sponsor or co-sponsor. Sponsorship means guaranteed advertising space, and sometimes cash to help with operating expenses. This week's sponsorships include the World Wine Festival, the American Indian Art Festival and Market, an exhibit at Science Place, *Dracula the Vampire* at the Dallas Children's Theatre, the *Marriage of Figaro* at the Dallas Opera, a Corot to Monet exhibit at the art museum, a classical music series at Myerson Hall, and five plays at the Undermain Theatre Ensemble.

This year, *The News* is giving $3.2 million in guaranteed advertising space and cash to nearly a hundred local groups, an increase of twenty per cent over the previous year, and of 200 percent over the average of the last four. Contributions to African-American and Hispanic groups have doubled, although in dollar amounts, by far the largest donations still go to the Dallas Symphony and Arboretum, the Starplex (which features rock and pop music concerts), the Dallas opera and art museum, Foley's Thanksgiving day parade, and the Cotton Bowl parade.

"Soft cost" is how Burl Osborne describes these sponsorships. "So long as we help in these other ways, we can't be faulted for not giving local groups all the news coverage they think they deserve. Sponsorship doesn't ensure news coverage; in fact, it may make it harder to get."

Twice a year, *The News* conducts a day-long media access seminar at which advice is given on how to write a press release. Just about anyone can attend, and editors freely hand out their own telephone numbers. An often quoted sentence in *The News'* policy manual reads: "Newspapers must combat the perception of being aloof, arrogant, and divorced from the community. Make every possible effort to obtain information from a caller or writer without referring them to another desk or person."

At these seminars, attendees receive a ten-page brochure titled "How to get your news in *The Dallas Morning News*," just as whenever a newcomer subscribes to *The News*, he or she is given a fourteen-page "owner's manual" which describes each of the paper's sections and features.

This Friday is the last night of high school football before the playoffs, and *The News* is keeping track of three hundred games. Five of these it is covering with its own staff writers; seventy more with stringers who will phone in their stories from a convenience store or car phone; the Associated Press has committed to send in scores on the rest. Rob Strope, a copy editor in the sports department, spends a full day each week making sure that nothing will fall through the cracks. Tonight, twenty men and women are waiting in the classified phone room to receive the stories that stringers call in. Crunch time is between 10:30 and 11:45 when the traffic reaches its peak.

Chris Perkins, the leading high school staff writer, is forty minutes away covering the Arlington/Weatherford game. Higher ranking teams are playing in the area, but the Arlington/Weatherford game will decide which team advances to the playoffs. Perkins prefers to cover a game where there is something at stake.

A native of San Antonio, Perkins has been covering high school football for eight years, six at the *Fort Worth Star-Telegram*, and two at *The Morning News*. He says he was sitting at his desk in Fort Worth one day when Dave Smith called. Dave said he had been reading Perkins' game stories, and was impressed. He added that *The News* wanted to "hire more black guys."

Perkins brings binoculars, a word processor, and a plug-in phone to the game. He keeps his own statistics and if unsure of a yardage gain or loss, checks with the *Times Herald* reporter who sits nearby. The game is still within Weatherford's reach until, with 4:53 remaining and Arlington leading by a touchdown, Weatherford tries a quarterback sneak on fourth down and is thrown for a loss. The momentum shifts and Arlington wins in a rout. With a minute still to play, Perkins goes down to the field. He waits through the obligatory post-game prayer, and then interviews the lineman who stopped the sneak.

"I felt it was then or never," the lineman says. "If I would have let them get past us, we wouldn't have made the playoffs."

Perkins waits outside the Weatherford locker room with a cluster of parents, but the door stays closed. "Coach must be still talking with his boys," someone says. His deadline approaching, Perkins climbs back up to the press box to finish his account of the game. It doesn't take long. Most of the story was written as the game progressed. It takes him less than a minute to send it back to the newsroom through a phone line.

Sunday, Perkins will be in the newsroom supervising player- of-the-week rankings. Tuesday, he will write a column filled with nuggets from this weekend's big games. Thursday, he will oversee play-off predictions. He says he likes his work. He understands how important it is. He likes to watch the cheerleaders and the dance teams, and he enjoys covering a game between schools of different races, to feel the emotion. He knows if he does a good job, Dave Smith will let him do a sidebar on a college or even Cowboys game. He knows that three of the school beat writers before him have been promoted into bigger jobs.

Saturday, November 9

On Saturday, Magic Johnson still dominates the news. On the front page is a color photograph of him with talk show host Arsenio Hall, next to a story by medical writer Rita Rubin that says President Bush hopes to take advantage of Johnson's superstar status to heighten AIDS awareness.

Inside is an editorial which says, "true to his upbeat nature, Mr. Johnson has decided to turn his setback into an opportunity." And in sports, Randy Galloway is taking Puritans to task for being more concerned with how Johnson got the disease than with his intention to crusade against it.

"If you want to pass moral judgment, fine," Galloway writes. "I don't. The sexual preference speculation that has already appeared in print is disgraceful, unprofessional, and gutless drivel."

Galloway's tirade is aimed at the *Herald's* Skip Bayless, who wrote yesterday there were rumors that Magic and his basketball buddies, Isiah

Thomas and Mark Aguirre, are bisexual. Bayless said he didn't believe the rumors. He was convinced Johnson acquired the disease through careless heterosexual contact. "As one of America's most eligible bachelors, Magic had a voracious sexual appetite," he wrote. But he repeated the rumors anyway.

On page one, beneath still another Magic Johnson story, is a report from Kathy Lewis in Rome. She writes that on the heels of Harris Wofford's upset in the Pennsylvania senatorial race, President Bush is pledging to propose a comprehensive health plan. On this trip, domestic concerns have kept intruding, she writes. At an unprecedented sunrise news conference, White House staffers seemed more anxious than usual. Later, Lewis said she had asked the President if, given the turmoil at home, he thought he should curtail his foreign travel. He told her no, but she hadn't included this anecdote in her story. It would have sounded like reporter intrusion, she later said.

Elsewhere on the front is a story by George Rodrique about the revival of hate groups in Germany, and another by Bruce Nicholson about the trial of the Houston woman convicted of hiring a hit man to kill the mother of her daughter's cheerleading rival.

At the bottom of the page is a story by Jonathan Eig and Olive Talley about Texas' growing psychiatric hospital scandal. On this one, *The News* is playing catch-up to the *Houston Chronicle* and one of the San Antonio papers. It wasn't until columnist Steve Blow got wind of the scandal that *The News* began covering it. Blow was a reporter, and the former East Texas bureau chief, before becoming a columnist. Although in his column he is prohibited from expressing political opinions, he occasionally manages to do so just by reporting the facts. In a column last month, he wrote about a seventy-three-year-old widower who admitted himself to an emergency room for chest pains, only to wake up the next morning a prisoner in an adjoining psychiatric ward. The man was held there until his insurance ran out. Several dozen people with knowledge of similar incidents wrote or telephoned Blow. Investigative reporter Talley and social services beat reporter Eig were then assigned to the larger story.

In the Today section, arts critic Janet Kutner reviews "Corot to Monet; the rise of landscape painting in France." This is an exhibit scheduled to open Sunday at the Dallas art museum, and earlier in the week, museum director Richard Brettel gave Kutner a personal tour. Her review, accompanied by color reproductions of three paintings, dominates the front page.

The Dallas art museum, reflecting the strengths and weaknesses of the city itself, has few Old Masters, but is well-endowed with Impressionist, Post-Impressionist, and contemporary paintings. The Corot to Monet exhibit plays to this strength, and Brettel had explained to Kutner how his approach to mounting the exhibit differed from that of other, less imaginative museum directors. In her review, however, Kutner chooses to emphasize how romantic landscapes became the precursor to impressionism.

Brettel will say later he was not entirely pleased. Yes, he appreciates the generous coverage *The Morning News* always gives the art museum. And yes, he sees the need for *The News* to write for a mainstream audience. But people in the mainstream will be coming to this exhibit anyway. Brettel's surveys show that to attract new people — people who wouldn't come to the museum otherwise — you have to challenge them with new ideas.

Dallas is a city of Protestant churches and in this respect more a part of the southeast than the southwest. The nation's largest Baptist church is here, and religion seems to play a role in most peoples' lives. *The News* always allots two pages to religious news in its Saturday paper. Included are stories about baby boomers rediscovering their religious roots, news briefs from around the country, and ads giving the time and place of church services.

Today's lead story is by Helen Parmley, the veteran religion writer, about a husband and wife who have a best-selling set of tapes and videos called Kids Praise. Parmley is also a member of the team assigned to cover air crashes and other disasters. She occasionally contributes to crime stories as well. In a front page story, she recently compared Easter to the World War II ballad, "I'll be seeing you (in all the old familiar places)."

"As in the song, there are not good-byes, no finality of a farewell."

If the Friday paper is heavy in entertainment news, the Saturday paper is heaviest in classified advertising. Classified is the most profitable of the three advertising categories, and dominance in classified is another big reason for *The News'* success.

In 1973, *The News* took the classified lead away from the *Times Herald*, and hasn't looked back since. Classified accounts for about forty per cent of newspaper advertising revenues nation-wide – up from about a third fifteen years ago. But at *The News*, classified's share of revenues is often ten per cent above the national average. By 1984, *The Morning News* was running more full-run classified advertising than any newspaper in the country. Some papers, the *Los Angeles Times* and *The Miami Herald*, for example, zone their classified advertising. They break part of it down into geographic segments, and charge a lesser rate. But not *The News*.

The reasons for *The News'* success in classified are many, including its morning advantage; a tough acceptance policy that gives its pages integrity (no adoption, no get-rich quick, no personal dating scheme ads); an equally tough abbreviations policy (*The News* refuses to accept any but the simplest abbreviations); a million-dollar promotion budget each year for radio and billboard advertising; a practice of training ad takers to be both generalists and specialists so in slack times no opportunities are missed; a willingness to pioneer in use of advertorials (see below); and a consistency in management philosophy. For twenty years, from 1966 until 1986, the paper had just one classified advertising director, Marvin Veal. Veal was then succeeded by two protégés, first Rick Starks, who later became director for all advertising, and then Eileen Dyer.

Veal says many newspapers operate on an *ad hoc* rather than consistent basis. Too often rates are cut to meet the competition. They reduce rates only for that portion of a customer's business in excess of what he or she ran in the month, quarter, or year before. If you are consistent, you don't lose your integrity, says Veal. And if you discourage a customer from placing an ad you know won't produce, you build repeat business.

Of these strategies, *The News'* policy on advertorials has stirred the most controversy. Advertorials, like infomercials on TV, take an uncritical look at some company, institution, or individual. Confusion and controversy result when a reader can't distinguish an advertorial from straight news reporting. When the two are positioned too close together, when both use the same or a similar typeface, or when the pages or sections in which the advertorial appears are not clearly labeled "advertising," problems arise.

Alex Jones, while media critic for *The New York Times*, criticized *The Morning News* for its use of advertorials. He said in an interview they were symptomatic of the paper's small town values. Advertorials *The News* allows would not be printed in an important newspaper on the East Coast. Len Foreman, former planning director of the *New York Times* company and now chief operating officer of the recently merged Newspaper Publishers' and Advertising Bureau associations, disagreed. He noted that the *Times* itself frequently runs advertorials. Well-produced advertorials are already a plus for newspapers, and likely to become more so.

If this is so, and it appears to be, *The News* is already ahead of the game. Its weekend papers are heavy in advertorial copy, appearing on the front of Friday's sixteen-page apartment seekers' guide, and on the front of Saturday's fifty-two-page automotive section. Advertorials will also be an important part of tomorrow's Sunday home section. Moreover, each section in which an advertorial appears carries a distinctive double band of blue, green, or orange at the top of the page. Each section is prominently labeled advertising, and is located in a part of the paper easily distinguished from regular news sections.

Most of the advertorials are in home and real estate sections, placed there in return for specific advertising commitments. Stories are rewritten from press releases and accompanied by photographs of the houses and developments described. The automotive section carries the next largest number of advertorials, but in employment there are scarcely any. In automotive, two of today's advertorials carry bylines. One is the account of the test drive of an Acura Legend written by Erika Sanchez.

Sanchez and two writers are responsible for writing the advertorials. They also write copy for most of the fifty special advertising sections *The News* publishes each year. These are also advertorials, though less obviously so. Titles range from this week's "SMU Homecoming" to "Volunteering" and various travel sections. By giving advertising (and occasionally the sports department) responsibility for writing special sections, "we help to preserve editorial integrity," said senior vice president, Harry Stanley. "It relieves the news department of having to write puff."

In 1981, the *Times Herald* gambled that its readers would benefit, and its advertisers wouldn't mind, if the *Herald* ran only straight news stories in the section where real estate ads appear. The *Los Angeles Times* had been able to do it. However, when *Herald* managers realized how much revenue they were losing and switched back, it was too late to recoup the market share they had lost.

On Saturday, by the time the 2:30 news meeting is held, most decisions with respect to Sunday's front page have already been made. Barring an international incident or some disaster, Saturday is seldom a day for major news. On Friday, Walt Stallings consulted with Bob Mong and selected a Magic Johnson analysis, a Hooked on Phonics story, and a Rodrique in Russia feature for Sunday's front page. Wire stories about a ranchers' feud in Montana and about political malaise in France are being used as filler in the early bulldog edition. These will be killed in later editions to make room for two stories from the state desk.

The first edition Sunday paper, called the bulldog, goes on sale in stores and racks throughout the Dallas area starting at noon Saturday. Only the A, metro, state, and sports sections are then updated for the remainder of the press run, which occurs early Sunday morning. Photographs run large in the bulldog, but smaller in later editions when there is more competition for space.

The News launched its bulldog edition in 1981. The *Herald* didn't respond until 1985, and by then it was too late.

Sunday, November 10

Sunday is the week's showcase newspaper. The stories are longer, better written, and less crisis-driven. *The News* sells 200,000 more copies on Sunday than on the average weekday.

Surveys show that readers spend twice as much time with their newspaper on Sunday. Sections are kept around the house or apartment longer and tend to be shared. Across the country, Sunday newspaper readership has trended upwards, however slightly, while daily readership continues to decline.

Today's paper includes more sports and comics pages, a commentary section called Sunday Reader, a weekly TV guide, both a *Parade* and locally produced magazine, travel and "High Profile" sections, and the week's heaviest accumulation of advertising. Classified accounts for ninety-six pages alone, and pages two through twenty-nine of the A section are filled with Dillard's, Foley's, and Macy's ads. There are relatively few preprints, however. *The News* encourages advertisers to use eight-page, standard size advertising sections called "we prints" instead.

"We prints" go to press later than preprints and can include a retailer's latest price changes. They are wrapped around news sections, and hence are less easily disposed of. They have the advantage of counting as in-paper advertising, and thus increase the percentage of space allotted to news content.

None of the five staff-written stories on today's front page have any relationship to yesterday's news events. All are what editors call "readers," meaning they are carefully crafted. Three of the five were finished and ready to go Friday, and all are accompanied by photographs and/or complicated graphics.

The lead story, from Anne Reifenberg in Washington, offers another look at Magic Johnson. By now the accepted belief is that he acquired the AIDS virus from a woman, and *The Morning News*, like most of the country, is breathing a sigh of relief.

"This was no emaciated Rock Hudson, silent about his predicament as he sought desperate treatment in Paris. No flamboyant Liberace, denying until the end what brought him down," writes Reifenburg. No, Johnson is the "epitome of American masculinity, a strapping thirty-two-year-old married father expecting his second child."

After Johnson's press conference, calls to the Washington AIDS office were up 500 per cent, most of them from heterosexuals trying to find out how they could be tested, she writes. A box on the front page refers readers to five more AIDS-related stories inside.

Above Reifenberg's story and stripped across the top of the page are two stories Stallings picked because he thought they would appeal to readers with widely different values. The first, by Doug Swanson on the state desk, is titled "Forbidden Relief: Ill people plead for U.S. sanctioned marijuana as government reviews drug's medicinal value." The second, a copyrighted story by Lee Hancock, also on the state desk, tells about a former gang member and twice-convicted felon awarded a license to operate homes for the mentally retarded in Fort Worth. Editors affix a copyright to stories likely to be picked up by other media without crediting their source.

Below the fold is Jeffrey Weiss' Hooked on Phonics story. Titled "Critics say Hooked on Phonics fails to live up to its promises," it is a sweeping, consumer-beware piece of a kind seldom found in *The Morning News*. "The cheery huckster's pitch seems to be everywhere . . . . Did you know there were only forty-four sounds in the English language? That's right forty-four." Weiss quotes a raft of detractors, including several of the region's leading educators. The story, which took a month to complete, continues for a full page inside and includes a five-by-five inch graph showing how the program works.

Consumer reporting is not a *Morning News* strength, and no doubt this is another reason for the paper's success with its advertisers. And since the people making Hooked on Phonics don't advertise in *The News*, it is a safe target. *The News* does have a small consumer complaint column (Line One), but it is anchored at the far back of the Today section. Consumer reporting, when it does occur, is usually intermittent and occasional, most often in Steve Blow's or business writer Scott Burns' column. Burns will offer advice on how to get your stock broker to stop churning, for instance, and Blow will occasionally go to the Better Business Bureau and compile a column listing the names of companies that receive the most complaints.

On the metro front a color photograph shows city council candidate Chris Luna standing surrounded by five new and prominent supporters. The picture tells readers all they need to know about Luna's chances in the runoff.

On the Texas and Southwest front, twinned stories by Sam Attlesey and Todd Gillman profile gubernatorial candidates David Duke and Edwin Edwards under the headline "Louisiana's fiery matchup."

On the front of the Today section are a pair of stories about sexual harassment – one written from a man's point of view, the other from a woman's. These stories gave editors cause for concern because neither met the standards normally insisted upon. The man's story is based on a single unnamed source; and the woman's is flawed both because her case is still unresolved, and because some of the important information also comes from an unnamed source. Confirming court documents were still to be obtained when the story was turned in, and the unnamed source still to be told that she ultimately could be identified. Mark Weinberg and Bill Evans, the two senior editors involved, would have preferred to hold the stories for further development. But because the stories were turned in late, and there were no good substitutes to choose from, Evans and Weinberg have had little choice but to apply some quick fixes and have the stories gone over by a lawyer.

Compounding their problem was the Today section's early deadline. In 1984, Burl Osborne discovered that if *The News* ran its presses straight instead of collect, the sports, metro, state, and A sections could have later deadlines and circulation would be able to deliver papers to homes and newsstands earlier as well. In a straight run, newspapers are produced twice as fast, but only half as many pages can be printed. In a slower collect run, sections of the paper are printed on separate presses and then mechanically collected. A collect run is not only slower, but it has less flexibility (and more waste) because sections have to be balanced in size. For *The News*, this meant classified advertising plus the Today section would have to be printed in advance, meaning a several hours' earlier deadline for classified and a day's earlier deadline for the Today section, but the tradeoff was worth it. With later deadlines, fewer makeovers (updates and corrections) would need to be made to hard news sections, resulting in reduced labor costs and less newsprint waste.

Despite this handicap of an earlier deadline, a comparatively small staff, and a reputation for attaching more importance to writing rather than hard news reporting skills, editors in the Today department had started raising their sights. The two harassment stories were bolder than the section's usual fare, and something of a pilot project. Editors had been told that occasionally lifestyle stories would be welcome on page one. In its long battle with the *Times Herald, The News* had seldom deviated from a page one philosophy of stressing the important and governmental, if sometimes dull, to the exclusion of lifestyle stories and lighter fare. "In a credibility fight, the dominant paper is going to be the one people believe, not necessarily the one they like," said Langer. Now, with the *Herald* fading, there was a subtle shifting of priorities, however. National surveys showed newspapers to be losing readers among working women, and there was concern that *The News* might be losing with them, too.

With the rise of the woman's movement, the Today section, like the women's sections at most large newspapers, had been transformed. At *The News*, it stopped being a section for homemakers and instead became a place for bright, trendy writing. "Too many of our people are still writing essays," said Mark Weinberg. "The lead gets buried ten paragraphs down. We're a newspaper, not a magazine."

Until recently, senior editors hadn't been concerned. Circulation continued to grow and the latest Belden survey (1988) showed that on Sundays, at least, the Today section had strong readership. The *Herald* might run more relationship, gender-related, women-in-the-marketplace kinds of stories, but the *Herald* was sinking. So what did that prove? *The News* had Fashion ! Dallas and Sunday's High Profile, and this same survey showed these sections still to be popular with women. "Research can tell you what a reader may think at a given moment," Osborne and Langer often said. "But it can't tell you what to put in the newspaper that will surprise or enchant them."

"One reason [Knight-Ridder's electronic] Vu-Text failed," added Langer, "was because people don't want to be specific about what they need. That only reinforces who you already are."

But as department stores changed ownership, and advertising support for Fashion ! Dallas and High Profile declined, business-side executives became concerned. "Our sports section is aimed primarily at men. So is our business section. Whatever it is that women do nowadays, we don't understand very well," said senior vice president Harry Stanley.

On today's business front are three stories about the proposed North American Free Trade Agreement and a column by Scott Burns on corporate greed.

The NAFTA stories are part of a continuing series by Richard Alm, whose beat is the world economy; Maggie Rivas, the border reporter in El Paso; and Mexico City bureau chief, Greg Katz. The stories are running on the business front rather than page one, Alm explains, because the treaty had still to be signed. There aren't any winners and losers yet. Today's stories are about opposition to NAFTA. Only in Canada is the resistance well organized, writes Alm. In Mexico, "the agreement can be likened to a train screaming along at 150 miles an hour when at the last instant someone asks it to stop," says Katz.

On its editorial page, *The News* strongly favors NAFTA, but also tighter border controls to stop the influx of illegal aliens. *The News* wants Dallas to become NAFTA's hub city, the Brussels of North America, as it were. Texas has the longest, most heavily populated border, and the bulk of the connecting highway and rail lines. A super-highway through Laredo now connects Dallas with Monterrey, the most dynamic of the Mexican cities.

Scott Burns' column is an attack on CEOs who take the same huge bonuses in good times and bad. Burns writes like he talks. He has a gift for making the complex sound simple. But, like Steve Blow, he occasionally runs afoul of senior editors by expressing a political opinion, at which point the offending sentence or paragraph is taken out. He says he has had only two columns killed, both on the subject of whether it makes sense for Dallas' rapid transit system to be based on the philosophy that the city center is fixed. Burns' contention is that because Dallas has no natural boundaries – no major river, ocean or mountain to bump against – the center of town is moving irretriev-ably northward. This isn't a message that Robert Decherd and Burl Osborne – convinced that a revitalized downtown is one key to Dallas realizing its potential as the pre-eminent middle American city – want to hear.

Burns didn't appreciate having two of his columns killed, but he said *The News* is such a good place in so many other ways – in find-ing jobs for people with disabilities, in giving people who screw up a second chance, and in allowing people like himself to moonlight – that he couldn't get too upset. An MIT graduate and the former financial editor of the *Boston Herald*, Burns supplements his salary by con-ducting day-long workshops on personal investment strategies. Today a full-page house ad is promoting his work:

"In a slow week, Scott Burns fields 250 phone calls, talks to 15 financial forecasters, peruses 27 savings plans and 309 newsletters, and reviews mutual funds, mathematical models, and merit-worthy mortgage rates."

In the Sunday Reader, Pederson's lead editorial is in the form of a letter explaining why *The News* opposed a collective bargaining agreement for Dallas police officers.

"Voters correctly recognized that enhanced power for one police union had nothing to do with effective crime fighting. . . . Rather than improve conditions . . . this labor negotiating tool could have left officers and administrators constantly at odds. . . . By rejecting collective bargaining, voters provided Chief Rathburn with a mandate to establish his own plan to reduce spiraling crime."

A second editorial notes that in winning the mayoral election, Steve Bartlett "not only received overwhelming support in his former North Dallas congressional district, but developed a breadth of support that should serve the city well in the 'new Dallas.' This support . . . sends a message to other council members that while each represents a district constituency, Mr. Bartlett represents the city as a whole."

Opposite the editorials is a page filled with letters of response to the Peirce Report. All are complementary except for one in which the writer complains that Peirce assigned no role for the city's churches to play. On the next page is an interview with Suzanne Garment, author of the book, *Scandal: The Culture of Mistrust in American Politics.* Carolyn Barta, editor of the Viewpoints page, asks whether there is more scandal in government now, or if it is only that America's appetite for the salacious had grown.

The News goes out of its way to downplay the scandalous and the salacious. When William Kennedy Smith was accused of raping a woman in Palm Beach earlier this year, the first story was page one news in New York and London, but *The News* played it small on page seven of its "A" section. Dallas' seamy side is left for the weekly *Dallas Observer* to chronicle.

There follow two book review pages offering five major and six mini reviews. Reviewers are a mix of writers from the paper (often Paula

LaRocque, Carolyn Barta, or Craig Flournoy), local pundit Philip Seib, and nationally known authors like Rick Bass or Alan Cheuse. Book editor Robert Compton says he sees his pages becoming more like *The Washington Post's* "Book World," where reviewers tell what the book is about then add some insight of their own, than like *The New York Times'* Sunday section, where essay writing tends to predominate. Today's reviews include a book about sports by Dan Jenkins and another by Thomas and Mary Edsall about what's been happening inside the Democratic party.

Sunday is when High Profile and the travel section appear, for which Lennox Samuels is responsible. Samuels oversees these two sections, plus Fashion ! Dallas, *Dallas Life Magazine* and House and Garden. Of the five, only the Travel and House and Garden sections are profitable, and Samuel's mandate is to revitalize the other three. His heritage is British and Caribbean and he has earned a reputation as a troubleshooter. Next to *Dallas Life Magazine*, which lost two million dollars last year, his biggest challenge is High Profile.

Begun in 1981 under the aegis of Ellen Kampinsky and Mark Weinberg, High Profile was conceived as way to add zest to the Sunday paper. Given the success of Wednesday's Fashion ! Dallas section, Osborne initially favored a second fashion section on Sunday. But Kampinsky urged a combination of *People*, *W*, and *Interview* magazines instead, and her vision prevailed. Each High Profile featured a life profile of a Dallas or Texas personality beneath a half-page color photograph. Inside were other, shorter profiles and a page of society news with the emphasis on fund-raising events. The people written about were movers and shakers and their beautiful wives (sometimes the beautiful wife before the mover and shaker), plus others, less well-known, who gave large amounts of money to charity. Although bad patches in a person's life were (and are) mentioned, the profiles were (and are) invariably positive in tone. From the outset, advertising support was phenomenal. Until the recession hit, Neiman Marcus, Bloomingdales, and Saks Fifth Avenue advertised in every issue, as did most of Dallas' upscale boutiques.

In 1985, *Adweek* magazine named Robert Decherd its newspaper executive of the year. In an interview, Decherd talked about the importance of High Profile.

"It's an example of where Burl looked at the data and said, 'If we have a group of readers with such demographic characteristics and certain buying habits and social interests and they would respond to a news section that talks about their world, what's wrong with that?' Many editors would have backed off. They would have said 'I don't want to do that because I'm not comfortable in that world' or 'I don't think that's a serious world.' Well, this is Dallas, Texas, and to fail to acknowledge that world is to fail to recognize a part of our city."

During the Dallas boom years, High Profile often ran to thirty pages, most of them advertising. Today, the page count is down to six. Samuels has begun revitalizing the section by shortening the profiles, broadening the subject mix, and recruiting reporters from metro, state, and sports desks to do some of the writing. Society photographs are no longer posed, but candid. The policy of not including *Morning News* or Belo executives in photos has been reinforced.

Today the lead profile is of Albert Achilles Taliaferro, an Episcopal priest, modern day guru, and confidant of country music singer Willie Nelson. Inside is a story about the Junior League in which reporter Kimberly Goad writes: "At seventy, the dowager of Dallas do-gooding has come of age. Now, anyone can be a Junior Leaguer." Prominently mentioned in the story is Matilda Robinson, an African-American woman who had been counseling the League on how to broaden its membership. I called Mrs. Robinson and asked if she agreed with what had been written and, after a short pause, she said that she did.

Leading the travel section, under the title "A tale of three cities: St. Petersburg, Stockholm, and Helsinki," are two stories and three photographs written and taken by Samuels himself. *The News* paid for Samuels' trip, as it does for such trips by all staffers now. Regular contributors to the travel section are former *News* editor Tom Simmons and his wife Jean, the former travel editor, both in their seventies.

Dallas Life Magazine features a ten-page photo essay by David Woo, about a local AIDS survivor. "This is not a man who looks like he should have been dead ten years ago," Russell Smith's accompanying story begins. "Tall and lanky, with intense dark eyes, he has a face that's fuller lately thanks to new dentures."

Lately, most newspapers have been losing money on locally produced Sunday magazines, and so have been phasing them out. So far, *The News* has resisted the trend. *Dallas Life* serves as a showcase for some of *The News'* best photographers and writers. *Dallas Life* has a four-week advance deadline. That today's issue would feature a photo essay about an AIDS survivor four days after Magic Johnson announced he has the virus is pure coincidence.

The Sunday TV book contains listings for eleven local, and nineteen cable, stations. It is about to be expanded to include dozens more. The more the television industry fragments, the better opportunity newspapers will have to build on their unique strengths, said Osborne.

In Plano, twenty-five miles to the north, the circulation department is experimenting with Sunday mail, an alternate delivery service that uses a second team of adult carriers to distribute catalogs, magazines, and product samples. Sunday mail is designed to reach up to 50,000 households, but so far results have been disappointing. Homeowners object to having plastic bags hung on their doorknobs, and most advertisers say the area is too small to justify all the paperwork involved.

Meanwhile four reporters, two columnists, and two photographers are at the Astrodome in Houston preparing to cover the Cowboys-Oilers game. For Dallas, this will be the first of three out-of-town games against potential Superbowl contenders. (The Redskins and Eagles are next.) Coach Jimmy Johnson had said his 6–3 Cowboys must win at least one of these games to have a chance of getting into the playoffs. (They win the next two.)

The Oilers are nine-point favorites, and the contingent from *The News* is pessimistic. On today's sports front, Rick Gosselin predicts that in a game matching two of the NFL's most explosive offenses, the Cowboys will lose. Randy Galloway questions Johnson's decision to start the game with five rookies.

But the Cowboys block the Oilers' first two punts, and jump to a 10–0 lead. Houston comes back in the second and third quarters to tie the game at 13–13. Each team scores ten points in the fourth quarter and the game goes into overtime. The Cowboys appear to have the game won when on an early possession they drive deep into Houston territory. But then, with the ball within field goal range, Johnson opts for one more play. He wants to get closer and be sure. Emmitt Smith carries the ball and for the first time all season he fumbles. Houston recovers and eleven plays later kicks a field goal to win.

In his wrap-up story, Gosselin says the Cowboys made enough good plays to deserve the victory. Galloway defends Johnson's decision to go the few extra yards that would have guaranteed a field goal. Kevin Blackistone, the other columnist at the game, leaves the press box before the game is over and stands behind the Cowboys' bench. Blackistone is a member of Dave Smith's "mod squad." Other members are Cathy Harasta and Kevin Sherrington, a gifted stylist.

"Emmitt Smith rose slowly," Blackistone writes. "He glanced at the ground. He looked at the sky. Then he began his slow walk back to the sideline.

"He stared straight ahead, at nothing, as he walked. It seemed an eternity before he finally made his way back to the bench after his fumble. Streams of sweat cut across his face. They looked like tears.

"Coach Jimmy Johnson applauded his star running back and nodded, as if to tell him it was all right. He patted Smith on the shoulder as he trudged past.

"Smith seated himself near no one on the bench.

"Cowboys corner back Isaac Holt was one of the first to come to him. He took a seat at Smith's left. 'There was no way I could tell him how to feel,' Holt said. 'It happens to all the great ones.'

"Moments later, as the Oilers started their march to a winning field goal, tight end Alfredo Roberts eased into the seat on Smith's right.

" 'I just told him to hang in there,' Roberts said. 'I told him he didn't have nothing to be ashamed of.' "

In Dallas, Mike Hashimoto edits the game stories before passing them on to the copy desk for a further check. To Gosselin's story, he adds a colorful phrase and a sentence of clarification. Gosselin is such an Xs and Os kind of guy that sometimes he writes above readers' heads. From Galloway's column, he takes out several of the "ands" and "buts" Randy likes to start his sentences with. Galloway writes too much like he talks. In Blackistone's column, he rearranges a paragraph or two. Blackistone is a recent transfer from the business news department. He's still new to column writing and welcomes the help, Hashimoto said.

Tomorrow, leading page one, will be Judy Walgren's color photograph of Emmitt Smith sitting dejectedly on the Cowboys' bench. The night editor had planned to use a second staff photo on the sports front, but Dave Smith called in and said no. Although staff photos normally take precedence over wire service photos, neither of *The News'* photographers had caught Emmitt Smith fumbling the ball.

Leading tomorrow's sports front will be an AP photo of Smith's fumble. A six-column headline in a glitzy shadow box typeface will read "Cowboys lose their grip."

Reaction to the Week

After observing a week in the life of *The News*, I went out into the community and talked with some of the people affected by the coverage.

Jimmy Johnson took time out from his team's practice at Valley Ranch to say he hadn't liked the cute headline – "Cowboys lose their grip" – that led Monday's sports front. Emmitt Smith was still sensitive about his fumble, and the photographs and headline made it seem as if the game had just that one play.

But then Johnson softened. He said sports coverage in Dallas was more positive than sports coverage in Miami and Fort Lauderdale had been (where he won a national championship coaching the University of Miami Hurricanes). "I read every word written about the Cowboys, and sometimes use the newspaper to send my players a message. I tell a player something and he may not listen. But if he reads it in the paper and his friends get on him, he may pay more attention."

Johnson said he doesn't hesitate to call Dave Smith if he has a problem, but so far he's done so only twice, most recently when an inexperienced columnist wrote that the Cowboys used the injured reserve list to hide unneeded players from other teams. Johnson was furious because he hadn't been interviewed before the column ran. "It looked as if we were the only team in the NFL that did such things."

Smith's reaction was to have his young columnist talk with Johnson to make sure they could continue working together. The columnist did, and they have.

Johnson described Randy Galloway as "very opinionated," but "even when I disagree with him, I at least find him interesting." He said he considered himself fortunate to have a beat writer as knowledgeable as Rick Gosselin.

The week after Magic Johnson announced he had the AIDS virus, Ralph Langer observed that *The News* had been emphasizing all the positives and none of the negatives about Johnson's predicament. "We've been playing it like he's a national hero." So, Kevin Merida suggested that sports do a take-out on the temptations groupies pose to an NBA rookie, and Dave Smith asked Kevin Blackistone to do a column on the perils of promiscuity. Blackistone's column, which ran a day later, compared E. J. (Earvin Johnson) to C. J., the Dallas woman who sparked a national furor by claiming she contracted the AIDS virus from a man, and now was having indiscriminate sex with lots more of them to get even.

"Magic is like C. J. except that Johnson's story is no hoax," Blackistone wrote. "Magic is like C. J., not by design, but by accident. Johnson is like any of the thousands of people who carry the AIDS virus, but don't know it. The paradox is that for a man, sexual promiscuity is considered a virtue. For a woman, it's a badge of shame."

Later, Blackie Sherrod would write:

"There is a strong hunch that the Lakers and the NBA and the Olympic Committee wish that Magic would stay retired and remain on his pedestal. He must be aware of that and, if so, why in heaven's name would he resolve to return? He doesn't need the money, does he need the attention all that much?

"Man, I don't know. I really don't know."

I didn't hear anyone criticize *The News* for the way it handled the Magic Johnson story. Several years earlier, *The News* had made coverage of the AIDS crisis a high priority.

Bob Ray Sanders, a radio talk show host and the city's most visible black moderate, blamed the *Times Herald* for sensationalizing the story, but not *The News*. Kay Vinson, a spokesperson for the gay and lesbian community, agreed. She praised *The News* for its sensitivity in covering Magic Johnson, and Lawrence Young for his pre-election story about gay and lesbian endorsements. The important thing, as Young perceived, was not that mayor-elect Bartlett wanted nothing to do with gays and lesbians, but that, for the first time, most of the other candidates did. Vinson only wished that *The News* had someone openly gay or lesbian in middle or upper management who could screen and suggest stories.

Bill Evans' response was that he hoped someone gay or lesbian already on staff would soon elect to be open about his or her sexual orientation. A few months later, this happened.

Reaction to *The News'* political coverage was more critical.

Monica Smith, who runs the (predominantly white) Dallas police association and led the campaign for a police officers' union said she couldn't even get *The News'* editorial board to listen to her arguments. She did praise *The News* for supporting "mothers against drunk driving," "buckle-up Dallas," and "victims who want to tell their stories" campaigns. But she complained that police officers were held to a higher standard than firefighters. Bill Evans replied, "We hold police officers to a higher standard because they are the only civil body authorized to kill when necessary."

In run-off elections for city council, a white and a white-supported black candidate won in two of the five majority black districts. Thanks to a disproportionately large number of white votes, Diane Ragsdale was narrowly defeated in one of these districts. Black leaders, sobered by their inability to get out a bigger vote, criticized *The News* for failing to endorse either of the two black incumbents.

"*The Morning News* is never satisfied with the leaders the minority community chooses for itself," Bob Ray Sanders said. "You don't see in-depth coverage of these people. You hear about them only during their most frustrating hour. Then they are covered prominently on the front page, and editorialized against."

"Diane spoke for people who felt they were not being heard," added Zan Holmes, a prominent black minister. "For people who make the most noise because they are hurting the most. These people are still hurting, and as long as they are, Dallas will experience pain and turmoil. Diane's loss is going to make our people even more bitter. Redistricting was supposed to help, but we don't have the organizational skills to compete with major white opposition.

"*The Morning News* has come a long way, but it still has a long way to go."

Edward Rincon, a marketing researcher who occasionally writes an article for *The News*' Op Ed page, criticized the paper for creating news it then turns around and writes about. He cited two polls done by *The News*' research department: one that distorted Hispanic views by concentrating only on *barrio* Hispanics, and another that showed mayoral candidate Steve Bartlett to have an insurmountable lead over an unannounced candidate, who subsequently chose not to run.

Hispanics, who easily gained two seats on the new city council, were, if anything, more outspoken than were the African-Americans.

"It's our turn now," several said. "For too long, the blacks have told us we'll take the chief's job, you can be the deputy. You haven't suffered like we have. You can always go back to Mexico."

Mexican Consul-General Oliver Farres, who made a practice of meeting regularly with *The News*' Bill Evans and Jim Landers, praised the paper for its recent coverage of Mexico, and of the proposed North American Free Trade Agreement. But Mexican-Americans in Dallas were more critical. They saw Belo's Channel 8 as friendlier to them than *The Morning News*. On Channel 8, they had an everyday anchor in Gloria Campos with whom they could identify and feel proud. Channel 8 had been Dallas' first network station to simulcast news programs in Spanish. Channel 8 didn't insist that everyone speak English. And it didn't run editorials saying a wall should be built along the U.S./Mexico border.

Ostensibly, Adelfa Callejo and Cipriano Muñoz have little in common. Callejo is a millionaire attorney and a power in state-wide Democratic politics. Muñoz is a Republican, leader of the Hispanic Chamber of Commerce, and served as co-chairman of Mayor Bartlett's successful election campaign. He would become chairman of Bartlett's Dallas-Mexico partnership and play a leading role in getting Mexican business leaders to choose Dallas over San Antonio and Houston as their sister city of choice. Both Muñoz and Callejo, however, accused *The News* of hypocrisy in refusing to endorse outspoken minority candidates for City Council while continuing to support white incumbents who had been equally divisive.

Callejo said the people running *The News* still refuse to criticize other whites. She is often asked to speak before white business groups about "the Hispanic perspective," but said that when she finishes, there is always silence, no questions, no attempt at dialogue. "It's as if the white leaders are afraid to know us as we really are."

Muñoz noted that Mexican-Americans are different from other Hispanics, and especially different from Cuban-Americans. "Many of the Cubans were professionals before they left Cuba. They knew how to access the system. The Mexican-Americans are the sons and daughters of migrant and construction workers. We don't want to be part of the mainstream if it means abandoning the friends and relatives we left behind.

"The only difference between us and the African-Americans is that they wore chains. We're tired of hearing that because many Hispanics have lighter skin, they can assimilate. That the only way to make it is to mainstream."

Muñoz and others said because of the nearness of Mexico and the ease of going back and forth, Mexican-Americans retain closer ties with their ancestral homeland than other immigrant groups. Mexican-Americans are neither expatriates nor immigrants, but something in between (an expatriate being someone still mainly nourished by the world left behind; an immigrant someone making himself over in a new country). They complained that the only Mexican-Americans readers of *The Morning News* usually hear about are those willing to adopt the values of the white middle class. A recent profile in *The News* of Texas' attorney general makes the point.

"The youthful, bespectacled [Dan Morales] is a Harvard-educated lawyer from San Antonio with a passion for public service. . . . He jogs, averaging five miles a day, several days a week. Other than these brief respites, however, he is single-minded in his professional dedication. He works twelve hours a day during the week, logs a few more hours on weekends, and hasn't taken a vacation in years."

"The only political candidates *The Morning News* favors are gringo-ized candidates," said Yolette Garcia, executive producer of Dallas' public TV station.

Rene Castilla, board chairman of the Dallas city schools, complained that reporters assigned to cover local government too often concentrate on the squabbling and infighting at meetings to the exclusion of larger issues. "*The Morning News* doesn't understand that in a majority/minority city, activists will be elected to the school board. And that in an urban democracy, arguing, emotion, and even confrontation aren't always bad. There isn't an urban school system in the country that isn't having problems. *The News* could help us find solutions by comparing Dallas' situation with that of cities facing similar problems."

In Austin, Bill Cryer, press secretary for Governor Ann Richards, praised *The News* for doing the best job of covering state government. "Like the *Houston Chronicle*, *The News* covers all the trees, but unlike the *Chronicle*, it often steps back and takes a look at the forest as well." He described Austin bureau chief Wayne Slater as "a terrier – here, there and everywhere," and political writer Sam Attlesey as "a bloodhound. Sam sits in the back of the house and after a while the veteran legislators come back and tell him things."

Cryer added that *The News'* computer analysis of campaign contributions had enabled it to become the state's pacesetter on ethical questions. But he said *The News* sometimes devotes so many columns and pages to a single issue that there's never enough time to get through it all. And he added that the paper is "all but invisible" when it comes to covering Hispanic issues. The Governor has to rely on the San Antonio papers for that.

In 1990, Commerce Secretary Robert Mosbacher refused to adjust the U.S. census to correct an acknowledged undercount of five million people, the vast majority of them minorities. In Texas, the undercount was five hundred thousand, and mostly Hispanic. *The News* supported Mosbacher's decision, although it cost the state a congressional seat and a billion dollars in federal funds.

The News describes itself as "Texas' leading newspaper," and prides itself on "delivery to twenty states, with same day delivery to cities on the East Coast." Yet it is still not possible to get same day editions of the paper in Texas' border cities of Brownsville, Harlingen, Laredo, and El Paso.

Not surprisingly, newsmakers in the white community were more complimentary. Dallas business and civic leader Charles T. Terrill said: *"The News* has become Texas' power newspaper. You do something good and you want to be in it. You do something bad, and you don't. But it's not so predictable anymore. You can't be sure who they're going to endorse." Former mayor Jack Evans praised *The News* for covering a difficult and controversial local election in a careful, measured way. Even when their remarks were critical, none of the people I interviewed seemed to think they might be punished if their comments became known.

DEMISE OF THE
TIMES HERALD

Death of the *Times Herald*

On December 8, 1991, a month after
the city council and mayoral elections,
the *Dallas Times Herald* announced
it was closing its doors and selling its
assets to *The Morning News*.

Now much that had seemed puzzling became clear: *The News'* caution
in covering the elections, its concern
not to offend anyone who could block
the sale, its recent increase in community sponsorships among black and
Hispanic groups, a policy change in
advertising long sought by car dealers, a tighter returns policy in circulation so as not to appear to be forcing
the *Herald's* hand, an earlier decision
to convert seven suburban dailies to
weeklies so Belo would look less like a
media monopoly.

One decision that didn't seem to
fit the pattern was a resumption of
the "Abuse of Authority" series two
weeks before the *Herald* made its announcement. At that point, the Justice
Department still hadn't approved sale
of the *Herald's* assets to *The News*,

and the series was critical of the Justice Department's civil rights division. Osborne said Ralph Langer had not known about the secret preparations for the *Herald's* demise; that at *The News*, only he and Halbreich did.

Two hours after John Buzzetta, the *Herald's* publisher, issued a press release saying his newspaper was closing, Robert Decherd announced that *The News* was buying the *Herald's* presses, subscriber list, and its building on Pacific Avenue for $55 million. Decherd noted that few communities have more than one newspaper anymore. A month earlier, Little Rock's *Arkansas Gazette* had closed and sold its assets to the *Arkansas Democrat*. Similar closings had occurred earlier in Los Angeles, Philadelphia, Baltimore, and Washington, D.C. Decherd defended his decision not to enter into a joint operating agreement with the *Herald*.

"There was no economic benefit or incentive whatsoever for us. . . . Philosophically, would we have liked to preserve two editorial voices? Of course, we would. But the costs to our shareholders and the adverse effect on *The News* I think were far beyond what that trade-off merits." Belo's analysis showed that *The News* could make more money competing against the *Times Herald* than it could through a joint operating agreement.

Decherd added that even with the *Herald* gone, there was more competition among network and cable television stations, radio stations, and direct mail in the area than there was thirty years ago. Asked what *The News* had done right, he replied they had capitalized on its morning advantage and its heritage as a newspaper of record serving larger community needs. *The News* had also developed what he called franchises: dominance on Sunday, and in business, sports, and international news.

Asked what he thought the *Herald* had done wrong, he was more circumspect. "When Times Mirror sold the *Times Herald* to Dean Singleton in 1985, you ceased to have two parent companies of comparable financial wherewithal. Singleton bought the paper at an inflated price, at a time when Wall Street was lending freely, even wildly, for acquisitions of media companies. Had the *Herald* been sold at an appropriate price to an institution or individual with staying power, it could have published longer."

Decherd asked Osborne to elaborate and Osborne said what *The News* had done "and would continue to do, was publish a newspaper independent of competitive considerations. It would not be reactive. . . . That suggests that our levels of service have to be higher than anyone else's, that the volume and range of our content has to be better than anyone is providing, and that our people have to be experienced and expert in the fields they are covering. It suggests the need to be present and competitive in the community, in terms of supporting arts and cultural and educational and civic activities and institutions. We're going to continue doing that. We're going to think more about it now than we did before. And that suggests additional space in our newspaper. . . additional features and columns . . . and even greater attempts to achieve diversity in what we publish, greater diversity in our newsroom and in every department of our newspaper."

If anyone thought Osborne was going to relax now that the newspaper war was over, they were mistaken.

Decherd said *The News'* cover price of twenty-five cents daily and a dollar on Sunday would remain the same. Advertising rates would go up fifteen per cent, less than the expected growth in readership and circulation.

There were no awkward moments. Everything went according to plan.

Times Mirror had sold the *Times Herald* to Dean Singleton, a native Texan, in 1985, the year after a collapse in oil and real estate prices sent Dallas into a recession. Singleton eliminated 100 jobs, killed the *Herald's* Sunday magazine, and closed its bureaus in Tyler, El Paso, Lubbock, and New York City. Then with the western half of the U.S. still in a slump, he boldly acquired the *Denver Post* and the *Houston Post*. This proved too ambitious a venture. So in 1988, pressed for cash and facing less determined competition in Denver and Houston than in Dallas, he sold the *Times Herald* to his associate, John Buzzetta. Before coming to Dallas, Buzzetta had been executive editor and then publisher of the *Patterson* (New Jersey) *News*. Like Singleton, Buzzetta was a protégé of Texas oilman and financier, Joe Allbritton.

Buzzetta continued to cut costs at the *Herald*, while gambling that the economy would recover in time for him to pay his creditors and the interest on the loans he had incurred. It didn't. By the time Buzzetta announced that the *Herald* was closing its doors, *The Morning News*, with a daily circulation of 428,000 and 642,000 on Sundays, had a two-to-one lead in circulation and sixty-five per cent of the two papers' advertising linage. And by then, most of the *Herald's* advertising and a third of its circulation was being sold at a discount.

No longer able to pay his bills, Buzzetta had two choices; declare bankruptcy, or sell his assets to Belo and *The Morning News*. If he declared bankruptcy, there would be no severance package for his employees, creditors would receive less on the dollar owed and, in the resulting confusion, many of the *Herald's* readers could be expected to give up on newspapers altogether.

Buzzetta first approached Belo in December, 1990, to ask if Decherd would consider a joint operating agreement, but Decherd said no. In May, Buzzetta approached Decherd again, this time to ask if Belo would be willing to buy the *Herald's* assets. This time the answer was yes and an offer was made, but because of an apparent misunderstanding, no deal resulted until August, when an agreement in principle was reached. The agreement in principle set the stage for a series of face-to-face meetings between Buzzetta and Belo president Jim Sheehan, to work out the details.

The two men got along. Both are bluff and plain-spoken, both from the urban northeast, both more comfortable working behind the scenes than in socializing with Dallas' movers and shakers. Buzzetta was born in Italy and grew up in Brooklyn and on Staten Island. Sheehan's grandparents came over from Ireland. The two men met from August to October, in one or the other's lawyer's offices (both conveniently located in the same building), or in a JoJo's coffee shop on Belt Line Road. Buzzetta often wore shorts, Sheehan jeans.

Once they agreed on details of the sale, the next step was to obtain the Justice Department's approval. In this, the primary responsibility was Buzzetta's. Buzzetta needed to convince the lawyers at Justice that Belo's was the only legitimate offer. And if it wasn't accepted, the *Herald* would have no choice but to declare bankruptcy. Under antitrust law, the seller must establish there are no other buyers before a direct competitor can buy a failing business.

Sheehan had to testify before the Justice Department only once. This meeting took place November 22, and Sheehan had to give his opinion as to why no other media company would be interested in buying the *Herald*, why the *Herald* couldn't be resurrected, and why there was no possibility of a joint operating agreement. Sheehan explained that publishing newspapers isn't like manufacturing widgets. If you cut back on the number of widgets you make, nothing much happens. But if a newspaper continues to lose circulation and hence readership, its ability to generate advertising revenue is permanently impaired. The issue was not how to preserve an ideal competitive situation, but how to deal with the fact that the *Herald* now had no choice but to close its doors. If allowed to buy the *Herald's* assets, *The News* would be softening the blow. The consumer would benefit by receiving continuous delivery of a daily newspaper, the *Herald's* creditors would be paid a substantial part of what they were owed, and 900 *Herald* employees would get a severance package they wouldn't receive otherwise. Asked what changes, if any, *The News* would make if the deal went through, Sheehan said *The News* would significantly diversify the range of opinions on its editorial pages.

Belo's case was strengthened by the fact that a few weeks before, the Justice Department had approved sale of the *Arkansas Gazette* to the *Arkansas Democrat*. The Gannett chain, which owned the *Gazette,* had been less meticulous in trying to find other buyers than the *Herald* had been. And since the price the smaller *Democrat* had paid for a monopoly in Little Rock was higher than the price Belo and the larger *Morning News* was offering in Dallas, *The News* would be buying on the cheap. This was additional proof, if more proof were needed, that the *Herald* had no other choice but to declare bankruptcy.

Still, the date for a decision came and went, and the Justice Department wasn't satisfied. It hired its own broker to approach possible buyers, but soon discovered, as Buzzetta had, that no one was interested. Finally, on Friday, December 8, the sale was approved.

What executives at *The News* now had to do was prepare to print 150,000 additional newspapers the night after the day the *Herald* ceased publication, and to make these preparations in the utmost secrecy. For if word of the *Herald's* imminent closure were to leak prematurely, who knew what might happen?

At *The News*, Osborne said only he and Halbreich had known about the secret negotiations. On Friday, after getting the Justice Department's approval, Decherd and Sheehan waited until after the market closed on Wall Street before walking across the street and briefing other key executives and department heads. At the *Herald*, Buzzetta kept the secret until shortly before 9:00 A.M. Sunday, when he issued a three-paragraph press release.

In Little Rock, the owner of the *Democrat* had refused to let the *Gazette* publish a final edition for fear of sabotage by angry staffers. In Dallas, the *Herald* did put out a final edition, although certain precautions were taken. Jeremy Halbreich and several *News* executives visited the *Herald's* plant on Sunday afternoon, but Osborne didn't go along for fear of rubbing salt in the wound. And on Sunday when Bill Evans briefed *The News'* reporters assigned to cover the story, he urged them to conduct themselves as if they were writing about a funeral.

Two stories about the *Herald's* closure led Monday's *Morning News*, but didn't dominate the page. Headlines on these and nine other stories inside read: "*Times Herald* shuts down today," "Closing of newspaper mourned across Dallas," "Publisher calls market too tough," "Staff expresses grief at publication's fate," "Demographic changes hurt," "TV weakened evening paper," "Civic leaders, residents lament loss," "Other papers seek to fill void," and "Belo's stock rises as Wall Street responds."

On an inside page, *The News'* Pat Baldwin and Robert Miller wrote: "The *Dallas Times Herald* rode to circulation heights through most of this century when America went to work in the morning, some-times before dawn, and came home to read its afternoon newspaper after supper.

"Mainly, it was a blue-collar world. It was a radio world. It was a world of eating at home and staying at home during the evening. . . .

"Although *The Dallas Morning News* historically had the largest overall circulation . . . the *Times Herald* proudly trumpeted until the early 80s that it had the largest circulation in Dallas and Dallas County."

The huge headline on the *Herald's* front page read "Goodbye Dallas."

A year before closure, *Herald* editor Roy Bode had asked Buzzetta to exclude him from any conversations about selling or closing the newspaper. Were he to know what was going to happen, he wouldn't have been able to manage the newsroom effectively, he said. As it was, aware that all indicators were trending downwards, he had been able to shrink his staff through attrition. "I never had to lay an em-ployee off in my four years as editor. Our last few months, we were filling only the essential positions."

Bode reserved extra space in the final edition for a list of all employ-ees and for three project stories that had yet to run. He solicited story ideas from everyone, not just the usual assigning editors, and made sure that all columnists were contacted and urged to write. He asked his Austin-based columnist Molly Ivins to strike several sentences from her final column that read: "*The Morning News* just had the money and the circulation. We ran the stories they were too chicken to print. . . . back when Blackie Sherrod ran the best sports department in Texas, it [the *Times Herald*] was a joy to read. [But we] lost Blackie to *The News*, of course, when the fools in management failed to give him enough money or honor. . . . I don't think they ever throw editors into swimming pools over at *The Morning News*. The *Herald*, at its best, stood for fun and justice. But management was never a strong point at the *Herald*." Bode said it was time to be gracious, and Ivins agreed.

(Later, she would write in *Mother Jones:* "Oddly enough, the *Herald* kept making money. But it was bought sequentially by two entrepreneurs who were leveraged up to their eyeballs, and every penny that the paper made went to pay off the interest on those debts. When you put no money back into a newspaper, it's a death sentence.")

Sports columnists Frank Luksa (whom *The News* would hire) and Skip Bayless (whom it would not) were on their way to Texas stadium to cover the Cowboys-Saints game when they heard the news. News day, their columns led the *Herald's* sports section under the headline, "Turn out the lights, the party's over."

On Monday, Osborne and Halbreich went from department to department at *The News* cautioning employees not to engage in victory celebrations. "How we behave the next few days can affect how we are perceived for years, perhaps decades, to come," Osborne said.

At the *Herald*, staffers continued the ritual begun Sunday of filling cardboard boxes with their belongings and filing past a security guard out the door.

Tuesday morning, with the help of many newly out-of-work *Herald* employees, Frank McKnight's circulation department delivered a *Morning News* to each of the *Herald's* 150,000 home delivery subscribers. McKnight had earlier put out the word that should the *Herald* go under, he would want to hire a number of its circulation people (he eventually hired thirty). He also let it be known that *Herald* retirees would receive free subscriptions to *The News* just as *The News'* retirees do. Tuesday's *Morning News* already contained one of the *Herald's* columnists (Ellen Goodman), and fifteen of its comic strips.

Each December, the chief executives of publicly-held newspaper companies meet in New York with Wall Street's securities analysts. Paine Webber had been hosting these get-togethers for nineteen years and they had become a way in which the industry measured itself. The sessions are held in a semicircular auditorium on Avenue of the Americas at 51st Street. Each company has an hour to tell its story and, as time allows, to answer questions. Depending on their interest in a given company, the analysts come and go, filling the seats, standing along the walls, or sprawling on the carpeted steps leading down to the podium.

As 1991 drew to a close, nearly everyone agreed that the year had been, as Tony Ridder, president of Knight-Ridder, put it, "the worst in the modern history of daily newspapers." Times Mirror announced it was reducing its payroll seven per cent, Gannett said it had had its toughest year since going public.

On a percentage basis newspapers reached half the households they had reached fifty years ago. CEOs feared that retail advertising was no longer in a cyclical downturn but in a permanent downsizing. Publishers were no longer able to maintain profit margins of twenty per cent by imposing advertising price increases higher than the rate of inflation. To compensate for shrinking ad revenues, most publishers had raised their daily cover price from twenty-five to thirty-five to fifty cents daily, and from $1.00 to $1.50 Sunday. Newspapers in thirteen cities had failed, or merged with stronger competitors. The industry was in trouble.

"I see lots of bruised reportorial egos as editors insist on tighter, brighter stories," Phil Meyer, a journalism professor at the University of North Carolina, told *The Washington Post*.

"We know how to win Pulitzers. We know how to topple politicians. . . . What we don't know how to do is get people to read serious journalism," added Knight-Ridder's Lou Heldman.

Each Paine Webber session was limited to an hour. If presenters chose to use all sixty minutes to tell their story, as several did, no one asked any questions. This year all the presentations were held to sixty minutes except the one for Belo.

Belo, the owner of just one daily newspaper (and five television stations) was among the smallest of the companies in attendance. Yet its presentation lasted for an hour and forty minutes. The analysts pressed Robert Decherd and Jim Sheehan to answer question after question.

How had *The News* been able to negotiate such an advantageous peace with its hated rival, they wanted to know. How had it been able to effect continuous delivery to the *Herald's* former subscribers? How much additional advertising revenue did *The News* expect to pick up? How had Belo arrived at a purchase price of $55 million? How was Decherd handling the public relations challenge?

Wall Street had not always been so kind or curious. It has a bias against companies with unpredictable earnings records and relatively few shares available to trade. Brokerage houses make their money on commissions, concentrate on short term results, and favor companies with which they do large amounts of business. Whereas two dozen analysts follow the newspaper giants – Gannett, Knight-Ridder, Times Mirror, and *The New York Times* and *The Washington Post* companies – normally scarcely a handful show an interest in little companies like Belo.

Jeffrey Russell, an analyst with SmithBarney, predicted that by ensuring continuous delivery, *The News* would retain at least fifty per cent (100,000 papers daily and 150,000 Sunday) of the *Herald's* circulation. This represented growth that would otherwise take the better part of a decade to achieve.

"It's an egg that can't be unscrambled."
–Jim Sheehan of the *Herald* acquisition

The Community Reacts

Reaction in Dallas to the death of *Times Herald* was, at first, surprisingly mild. Perhaps it was because the *Herald* had had so many publishers and editors over the last seventeen years that people had begun to lose count. Or because as the paper shrank in size and its headlines got bigger, blacker, and more sensational, many people had sensed that the end was near. No doubt it had a lot to do with the way Belo and *The Morning* News handled the transition: by guaranteeing next day delivery of *The News* to all former *Herald* subscribers, by increasing advertising rates only a modest amount, and by finding a home for all the *Herald's* comic strips, many of its columnists and best writers, and all of its community sponsorships.

W. A. Criswell, the legendary senior pastor of Dallas' First Baptist Church, the nation's largest, said he was not sorry to see the *Herald* go. "They were just down the street, but they never made an attempt to know me. Their reporting was often snide and sarcastic. *The Morning News* always tried to be fair." County Commissioner John Wiley Price, one of the news media's most vocal critics, said only that *The News'* editorial page had lately been trying to move to the center, while the *Times Herald* was moving to the right. And Jack Evans, a former mayor and former CEO of the Tom Thumb supermarket chain, said he didn't think the business community would be particularly upset. *The News* was likely to pick up the most valuable part of the *Herald's* readership. Advertisers now could save money by using one paper instead of two.

The upscale stores and boutiques which *The News* had convinced to be *News*-only advertisers appeared to be the most upset. They would have to pay now for additional circulation they had been told they didn't need.

D (for Dallas) magazine ran a cover story by Jim Schutze, the *Herald's* former metro columnist titled "It wasn't murder. Was it suicide?" Schutze said the *Herald's* circulation department had been able to write plenty of new orders, but was never able to get them delivered on time. He blamed poor business management and an arrogant and inconsistent news philosophy for his paper's demise.

"Between 1975 and 1985, the *Herald* won two Pulitzer Prizes, fielded nine Pulitzer finalists, won four Picture of the Year awards, two national Sigma Delta Chi awards, two Overseas Press Club awards, a World Press Club award, a George Nathan award, and a slew of others. . . . The sports section was consistently singled out for unparalleled investigative reporting.

"The problem was that, by 1985, these prizes were meaningless. . . . The war was already lost. . . . Robert Decherd and Burl Osborne had a strategy from which they never deviated." The owners of *The Morning News* were natives. "They knew the big things in their gut."

Dick Hitt, who in various incarnations spent thirty years at the *Times Herald*, wrote in *Texas Monthly:*

"When Tom Johnson, Ken Johnson, and Will Jarrett arrived in the mid-seventies to run the *Herald's* news operation. . . . [A] new brand of journalism (for Dallas at least) cut through decades of passivity and faintheartedness. It was hard-edged and sparkled like a sword – a double-edged sword, as it turned out.

"Dallas had never had a tough, neither-fear-nor-favor newspaper, and it wasn't ready for one. 'I think that was the beginning of the end,' says Frank Luksa, echoing a theory of many of his colleagues. 'It scared the city's leadership, having a paper that wouldn't do their bidding.'"

"The *Times Herald* started making all the lists of best papers, but it alienated the Dallas establishment with its aggressiveness and its 'outsiderness.' That perception was encouraged by *The Morning News*, which was getting its nose bloodied. *The News* followed its enemy in deciding to spend money to make money, and what resulted was the most intense newspaper war of the times. Tom Johnson's forbearance and Will Jarrett's minimalist management had made the *Times Herald* a columnist's delight."

Invariably, Tom Johnson gets the credit for creating the momentum that made the *Herald* into a very good newspaper. The executive editor of the *Herald* from 1973 to 1977, he left Dallas in 1977 to become first president and then publisher of the *Los Angeles Times*. He returned as the *Herald's* publisher in 1984/85 in an attempt to revive it, while still serving as publisher of the *Times*.

In a recent interview Johnson, who is now president of CNN, said he would never have left Dallas had he known what was going to happen at the *Times Herald*. "I was happy there. My children were happy. At the newspaper, we were doing exciting things." He credited Robert Decherd and Burl Osborne with inspired leadership in winning the newspaper war. But he also said Times Mirror and the *Times Herald* had made grievous mistakes. Failure to transform the *Herald* from an evening to an all-morning paper was one. "But our survey showed thirty per cent of our readers preferred an evening paper and would quit us if we did." Equally damaging had been the proliferation of publishers, editors, and circulation directors, each with a different idea of what needed to be done.

In the days following the *Herald's* demise, there were no organized outcries, no write-in campaigns urging that *The News* hire Molly Ivins or Skip Bayless, no petitions demanding that the paper, somehow, be magically revived. For a day or two after the announcement, radio talk show hosts were besieged by callers asking whether Belo had bought its competitor for the sole purpose of creating a monopoly. But the furor didn't last and the calls subsided.

But then in mid-December, Decherd, Sheehan, and Osborne took the Dallas area's five congressmen to breakfast at the downtown Tower Club. Democrat John Bryant said he would have opposed *The News'* purchase of the *Herald's* assets, and added that he intended to launch an inquiry at the Justice Department. Bryant and Republican Dick Armey complained that their congressional activities received scant coverage in what was now Dallas' only daily newspaper. (Soon *The News* added another reporter to its Washington bureau whose job would be to intensify coverage of Texas' congressional delegation.)

On December 19, the weekly *Dallas Observer* published a cover story by Laura Miller, a former star *Herald* reporter, titled "Who killed the *Times Herald?*" Miller accused Osborne of hypocrisy, and marketing vice president Harold Gaar of spin control. Their efforts, she said, were aimed at preventing the public from perceiving what really happened. The *Herald's* sudden death was due to *The News'* insatiable appetite for dominance. Calling Osborne the General Norman Schwartzkopf of the Dallas newspaper war, she described the Monday meeting at which he addressed newsroom staffers.

"Now with the corpse of a 112-year-old institution still warm, Osborne was explaining the new game plan. It was vintage *Morning News*, employees say. Vintage Burl.

"Here, as the city mourned, the Burl machine – which had given us feel-good news about Dallas and reassuring economic forecasts and the fawning prose of High Profile – was happily bubbling away with a new sales pitch.

"'There is to be no public gloating,' he declared. 'If we high-five and cheer, it will reflect badly on us.'"

Still, Miller, like Schutze, concluded that the moral was "you can't beat blood. . . . When Robert Decherd makes decisions for *The Morning News*, he is making them not just for himself and his shareholders, but for his children and grandchildren as well."

The *Dallas Observer*, an alternative free weekly with a claimed circulation of 85,000, had recently been purchased by New Times of Phoenix in anticipation of the *Herald's* demise. New Times was the publisher of similar, if fatter and more successful, weeklies in Phoenix, Denver, and Miami. The *Observer's* new editor was thirty-three-year-old Peter Elkind, formerly a staff writer with *Texas Monthly*. In his first issue, Elkind announced that he was starting Belo Watch, a weekly critique of Dallas' "multi-headed media Behemoth."

Meanwhile Richard Connor, publisher of the *Fort Worth Star-Telegram*, was also accusing Osborne and *The Morning News* of hypocrisy.

"The news business does not need one of its own to raise questions about credibility," he wrote. "But unless *The Dallas Morning News* hires the Dalai Lama as its spokesman, no one is going to believe how saddened its executives are at the prospect of a world without their friendly rival. So, let's dispense with the sad posturing, the bowed heads, the hands folded as if in prayer. Both newspapers set out to obliterate one another a decade ago, and now one is gone."

Connor warned *The News* to stay out of Tarrant County, where Fort Worth is located, and he hired Molly Ivins to write a front page opinion column for the *Star-Telegram*.

In an interview, Connor characterized *The Morning News* as "the last of the great cafeteria newspapers – too balanced and dull" to attract the flood of newcomers moving into the corridor between Dallas and Ft. Worth. He used a quote from Molly Ivins to illustrate the difference between his philosophy and Osborne's: "Objectivity has been a crippling goal in American journalism. We think if we can quote one side and then the other, the truth will be somewhere in between. I'd like to see newspapers stand for something. I'd like to see them raise a little hell."

The New York Times joined the fray two weeks later when it ran an article in its Sunday business section that asked whether the Justice Department hadn't "played dead" in allowing conservative newspapers in Little Rock and Dallas to gobble up their liberal competitors. "While the *Arkansas Gazette* and *Dallas Times Herald* may have died of natural economic causes, the circumstances are suspect," wrote Stephen R. Barnett, a law professor at the University of California at Berkeley. Barnett had previously published an article in *The Nation* attacking monopolies and opposing a proposed joint operating agreement between the *Detroit News* and *Detroit Free Press*.

In mid-January, the *Dallas Observer* ran a story saying that Dallas area congressman John Bryant, a Democrat, was launching an inquiry into the sale of the *Herald*. Bryant "wasn't necessarily angry at *The Morning News* for blowing away its cross-town rival." Nor was he angry at the *Times Herald* "which had seemed a little too eager to take the bullet." His wrath, he said, was directed at the U.S. Justice Department, which appeared not to have asked enough questions. The death of the *Times Herald* made Dallas the largest city in America without two daily newspapers. Since Belo already owned the area's dominant television station, "two or three people who live in the same part of town could now decide what we read and most of what we see on television. Had Justice demanded the *Herald* be offered for public sale, someone else might have bought it more cheaply."

Robert Decherd and Jim Sheehan appeared unconcerned.

Sheehan cited analyses showing that Belo had paid a rock bottom price for the *Herald's* assets. To gain immediate access to so many new readers had been worth the purchase price alone. The *Wall Street Journal*, in its coverage of the sale, tended to agree: "The price would appear to be a bargain for Belo. . . . By comparison, the *Arkansas Democrat* bought the assets of its Little Rock cross-town rival the *Arkansas Gazette*, a smaller newspaper in a smaller market, for $69 million in October."

Decherd said he was confident that when Channel 8's license came up for renewal by the Federal Communications Commission, there would be few problems. Yes, the FCC had ruled that after 1975 no company could own a newspaper and television station in the same market. But Belo had acquired its ABC affiliate in 1950, so the ruling didn't apply. Since 1975, the Dallas market had become more competitive. Direct mail and cable TV had made the influence of a single newspaper less dominant.

"We've tried to attack the toughest
problems first. That doesn't mean we've
finished the job."
– Burl Osborne

Turmoil in the Newsroom and Beyond

So long as the *Times Herald* was alive, *The News'* newsroom had a visible target against which it could measure itself. Reporters and editors could lock arms against a common enemy. A top-down management style was seldom criticized because there was a war to be won.

But by early 1992, reporters and some of their younger editors began turning inward. Personnel problems and prize winning became more important. Issues that had seemed mere irritants before now escalated in importance. Tougher questions began being asked.

Now that *The News* was a monopoly, would its reporters have to be even more cautious than before, for fear of offending somebody? Did the newsroom have too many layers of editors, and not enough people doing the real work? Had management gone out of its way to train and promote

African-Americans, and to the detriment of women and Hispanics?

The *Dallas Observer's* Belo Watch became a way for disgruntled staffers to ventilate their fears and angers. The *Observer* had begun running stories that *The News*, given its fairness standards and preference for positivism, couldn't or wouldn't print: a takeout on a homophobic demonstration at City Hall, a cover story titled "Inside the mess at the Dallas art museum," personal attacks on Ross Perot and other prominent Dallasites.

Belo Watch asked why, if *The News'* writing coach was so great, its reporters' stories were often so bland. It exposed a minor conflict of interest in *The News'* sports department, and questioned the paper's refusal to allow an *Observer* rack in front of its building. (The ban was eventually lifted.)

Peter Elkind, who writes Belo Watch and edits the *Observer*, said "*The News* presents all the crap and buries the real story. It is slow to make connections between powerful people and institutions, and makes everything seem rational, several steps removed from reality."

Suddenly, editors at *The News* found it wasn't so much fun being a winner anymore.

During the Gulf War in 1990, a story came in from George Rodrique in the eastern Mediterranean in which he profiled attack bomber pilots aboard the USS *Theodore Roosevelt* who had suffered the most casualties. Deep in his story was an account of briefings in the squadrons' ready room.

"To ensure attendance, these often begin with a motivational film – such as a woman taking off her bathing suit. 'This is to remind us of what we are fighting for,' a pilot said."

The story had been cleared by military censors.

Sarah Campbell, a copy editor on the desk that night, took offense. She considered the reference to pornographic movies sexist, and she asked news editor Walt Stallings to take it out. She said she had been told to be supersensitive to anything in any way offensive to African-Americans, and wanted to know why there wasn't a similar sensitivity towards women.

Stallings consulted with the night national editor and the night international editor, both men, and decided to leave the passage in. He agreed with Campbell that the paragraph was sexist, but thought it extremely revealing, and hence newsworthy. It showed the military to be acting in a way that wouldn't be tolerated in a civilian institution. The Navy might claim to be changing, but obviously it wasn't, as Rodrique had shown.

Campbell wasn't satisfied, nor were several of the other women on the desk that night. And so the next day, Stallings convened a copy editors' meeting, to which he invited Bob Mong and Bill Evans. He asked Campbell to voice her concerns, which she did, as did others, notably assistant news editor Shawna Seed.

Seed said her objection was not to the passage, but to the fact that it had been left in the story without comment, presumably as flavor. No attempt was made to highlight the passage, to view with alarm, or say "for God's sake, look what the Navy is getting away with."

In the ensuing discussion, other women complained that there were always more pictures of men on page one than there were of women. Stallings agreed, saying government stories are usually driven from the male point of view. Some women criticized management's insistence on formal titles. "Mr. is an okay title for men since it is neutral," they said. "But Ms. implies the woman is a feminist, Mrs. that she is a traditional homemaker, and nobody understands what Miss means anymore." The incident, although illustrative of management's willingness to listen, reinforced among many reporters a perception that *The News* was not prepared to change. The fact that this incident was still being discussed a year and a half later illustrated the depth of feeling.

On the Belo board of directors there was just one woman, Robert Decherd's older sister, and of *The News'* ten officers, only Rena Pederson was a woman. None of the newsroom's senior editors were women, and among its eight assistant managing editors, only two were women, and neither of these had a budget or people to supervise. Writing coach LaRocque, one of these two, was often perceived as a spokesperson for senior management.

In 1990, the newsroom had announced twelve promotions. Three African-American men were made assistant managing editors in positions that hadn't existed before; Gilbert Bailon, a Hispanic, was named metropolitan editor; and two men, Mark Weinberg and Lennox Samuels, were named to replace Ellen Kampinsky, who previously had been in charge of all the feature departments. Melissa Houtte, named assistant managing editor for Sunday, was the only woman promoted.

Kampinsky had asked for and been granted a leave of absence to go to art school. And at about this same time, three other women with potential for senior management (a foreign editor, national editor, and Today section editor) had left the paper, two of them to start families. A year later, two women department heads (business and Today sections) were, in essence, asked to return to reporting, where women often hold choice assignments. Now, the question being asked was whether women were being discouraged from seeking jobs in upper management, or whether they were electing to opt out. Was there something about a senior management job at *The News* that made it unattractive to a woman? This same question had been asked several years earlier when two women selected for the newspaper's executive training program failed to stay the course, but the questions remained unanswered.

Asked to comment, Robert Rose, the psychologist on retainer that senior editors use to interview people they want to hire, promote, or be counseled with, said "people who don't want to work odd, unusually long hours shouldn't go into management. Women often seek a more rounded life than men do. A woman will be having problems and be sent out to talk to me. She'll often say, 'I'm thirty-seven years old and don't have a life outside the newspaper.' Or, 'Mom and Dad don't rag on my brother about starting a family, but they do me.'"

Rose asks people about to be promoted who they will work for, and who will be working for them, so chemistry problems can be anticipated. He says editors are different from managers in other lines of work. "Scarcely any have a business background and few see themselves as managers first. Usually they are psychologically astute –

they wouldn't be editors if they weren't – but it's unlikely the thought of managing is what brought them in the door."

Many, however, have trouble talking with people face-to-face. Because they work with the written word, they often prefer to handle a problem with a memo they can write, edit, and leave on someone's desk. Too often, this leads to another carefully crafted memo, and the problem remains unsolved.

Two qualities Rose looks for in people seeking an editor's job are creativity and a high degree of energy, but he also likes to see an aptitude for caution and control.

Before she left the newspaper, Ellen Kampinsky made a report on job sharing to the Dallas/Fort Worth Association of Women Journalists. She showed that successful companies "are becoming responsive to people's needs rather than just job needs. Mothering is a fact of life, and I feel it is important to keep mothers in the job stream and moving up to the highest levels of management." She described a program that the *Seattle Times* uses for people who need to spend more time with their children.

But job sharing had yet to catch on at *The News*. "You can't have one person responsible Monday, Wednesday, and Friday, and someone else Tuesday, Thursday, and Saturday, and expect to have any consistency," Osborne said.

Yet with the demise of the *Times Herald*, pressures for change were building. Women staffers complained about an absence of role models. They said because few of *The News'* senior executives had wives who worked, that the men running the newspaper didn't understand today's woman very well. In a newsroom that prided itself on promotion from within, the last three women awarded management jobs – as Sunday editor, Today editor, and deputy business editor – had had to be recruited from outside.

Inside the building, women began speaking up.

"Bubba might still drive a pickup truck with a gun rack in the back," Maryln Schwartz wrote in her Today section column. "He might still think the day's weighty issue is that bikini-clad models are no longer politically correct in beer ads. But Bubba's wife has changed. She, who once spent her afternoons preparing barbecue dinners for Bubba, and selling cosmetics on the side, has taken the expertise learned in organizing charity event style shows and ladies' luncheon groups, and is running the local political precinct."

"My male bosses say 'Trust me. I'll take care of you. I'll make sure your views are represented,'" said Pam Maples, an assistant national editor. "But in this day and age that sounds patronizing."

Anne Riefenberg was single and a prize-winning reporter in the Washington bureau. She didn't yet aspire to be an editor, nor had she been having trouble getting choice assignments. But she, too, was concerned about the scarcity of women in upper management. "Flex time and job sharing are no longer just women's issues. The young married men are concerned now, too. Women, by not speaking up, have hurt themselves."

Carolyn Barta, a twenty-seven year veteran and former political editor, agreed. "We thought our bosses would find ways to keep us challenged. We didn't think it would be professional to complain. We can blame them, but maybe we should blame ourselves more. We should have been spelling out what our needs are."

"I applaud what they've done to hire and promote blacks," said Melissa Houtte. "It was long overdue. But if they'd been equally concerned about the needs of women, they wouldn't be in the fix they are in now."

"If they think those meetings our editors had with civil rights activists had nothing to do with all the black promotions, they're kidding themselves," said veteran reporter, Gayle Reaves.

"Texas is still a tough place for a woman who chooses a non-traditional path," added Lee Cullum, the former editorial page editor at the *Herald,* and now a contributing columnist at *The News.* "Dallas may look like a midwestern city – practical, hardworking, a get-up-early-in-the-morning kind of place. But when it comes to manners, Dallas is still very southern. When people aren't mannerly, we don't quite know how to act. Raw emotion is something this city has trouble dealing with. The blacks understand, and have taken advantage of this." Cullum's unspoken conclusion was that women, as yet, have not.

Dallas' large and fast-growing Mexican-American community is a relatively recent phenomenon, its growth triggered by the economic boom of the 1970s and early 1980s. Now with the economy recovering, its numbers are accelerating. Many of the newer arrivals are more comfortable speaking Spanish than English.

The News' strategy has been based on the assumption that Dallas is an English-oriented city with an English-speaking Hispanic population anxious to assimilate. "We talked about publishing some of the paper in Spanish, but concluded that it didn't make any sense," Osborne said. "In some neighborhoods, the Hispanics are far more assimilated than blacks. The same issues appear to be important to Hispanics as to the rest of us." Although the *Times Herald* would occasionally print stories in Spanish – some of its coverage of the Mexico City earthquake, for example – *The Morning News* had (and has) done nothing to encourage Spanish speaking. A recent editorial encouraging Dallas to become more of an international city had seemed to stress the importance of learning French instead. "Je Parle Dallas," it read. "New international school [sponsored by the French government] should be a big plus."

In 1989, sixteen prominent leaders from the Hispanic community met with Osborne and Rena Pederson for the purpose of encouraging *The News* to be more sensitive to Hispanic issues. They wanted to set themselves up as an advisory group with which editors would regularly consult. A second goal, unstated in advance, was to get associate editorial page editor Richard Estrada fired. Both attempts failed, and few members from the group had been back to the newspaper since.

Estrada continued to set the tone for *The News'* position on immigration issues. He feared that as Dallas's Hispanic community continued to grow, and Hispanics took jobs that otherwise might go to African-Americans, the racial atmosphere in the community would become increasingly volatile. "The reason employers prefer to hire Hispanics over African-Americans is no mystery," he said in an interview. "Even if the Hispanics know no English, most are free of an underclass stigma. Some have useful skills, and all are deferential, an attitude more attractive to employers."

Estrada – and *The News* – continued to advocate that a wall be built at strategic points along the U.S./Mexico border. As a result, many Mexican-Americans came to see him as a man who hated his own people.

Bilingual ballots "serve to reinforce the non-English speaker's native language and relieve the pressure on that individual to learn English," Estrada wrote in a recent column. "In the most extreme case, we need only to look at Lebanon, the Indian subcontinent, the former Soviet Union and Quebec to see where that can lead."

"The larger the ethnic immigrant cluster, the more prolonged and difficult will be the assimilation process," he added in another column. "If it is true that German immigrants eventually assimilated in America to the point where they are virtually indistinguishable from Americans of English descent, so too is it true that assimilation prevailed when the rate of German immigration declined."

Such talk was inflammatory to Mexican-Americans who wanted to Americanize, but not at the cost of abandoning their language and culture. A letter to the editor made the point:

"The Maginot Line mentality expressed in your recent editorial proposing concrete sunken fences, steel wired fences, agents armed to the teeth with the latest military equipment, all for the purpose of stopping illegal immigration from Mexico, is appropriate for a backwoods newspaper addressing a community of white supremacist Bubbas, but not for the only newspaper in a city striving to become a world-class international business and cultural center.

"What these hordes of illegal immigrants will do to your proposed border barricades is simply go around them. . . . It would take more troops than we have stationed in Europe to effectively patrol such a barricade."

In 1980, there had been one Spanish-speaking weekly newspaper in Dallas, one Spanish language radio station, and no Spanish language television stations. In 1992, there were six Spanish language weeklies, two Spanish language radio stations, and two Spanish language television stations.

Apart from metro editor Gilbert Bailon, neither *The News* nor Belo had any Hispanic executives. Soon, Chris Luna, one of the two newly elected Hispanics on the City Council, would convince other council members to cancel the city's $275,000 annual contract with *The News* to publish public notices. He, and they, said that neither *The News* nor Belo had enough minorities in senior management.

Many reporters feared that with the *Herald* gone, their editors would become more cautious than ever. They cited two incidents as examples of what they hoped would never happen again.

In 1990, *The News* had waited five days before reporting that County Commissioner John Wiley Price had promised "to take to the street with arms" if the city hired another "good ol' boy" police chief. Steve Blow had taped a conversation with Price on a Friday in preparation for a routine column the following week. In the course of their conversation, Price mentioned several recent police shootings, and became agitated. He said he would take to the streets with guns if the city hired another "good ol' boy" police chief.

At first Blow said he thought, "that's just John talking emotionally again." But then over the weekend, Blow found himself thinking that, since Price was black, it might be reverse racism for him to be so protective. Maybe this was a news story. Monday morning, Blow told his editors what had happened, and they assigned Pete Slover, a reporter on less friendly terms with the commissioner, to interview Price and make sure he had meant what he said. On Tuesday morning, Slover talked to Price.

"These statements are pretty strong," Slover said in a second taped interview. "And I wondered whether they should be taken literally or whether that's just sort of a figure of speech. How did you mean that?"

Price: "I meant it just like I said it. . . . If you bring in a good ol' boy in this system again, we're going to be in the streets. Physically, literally shooting folks. We're not going to tolerate it."

Price's secretary subsequently called *The News* and urged that the story not be printed. She said her boss wasn't himself and had been distraught. Stu Wilk then called Price and, in a third taped interview, again asked if the commissioner stood behind what he had said. Price said he did. On Wednesday, the story appeared on page one under a one-column headline: "City given warning by Price." Rena Pederson's editorial the same day called Price's statement outrageous.

"When he took the oath of office as county commissioner, Mr. Price swore to preserve, protect, and defend the constitution, the laws of the United States, and the laws of the state of Texas. In that sense, he has undermined his validity and credibility as an officer of government, and if he will not retract his call to violence, Mr. Price should step down from his position on the Commissioners Court."

The next day, in a second page one story, Price recanted.

When asked about the incident, Osborne said if Price had not been a member of the minority community, "we would not have waited. But he was and that made a difference. I'd do it the same way today."

Further investigation revealed that both the *Times Herald* and Belo's Channel 8 had heard Price make similar remarks, but elected not to go with the story until after *The Morning News* did.

A more frequently cited example of excessive caution was *The News'* delay in reporting Governor Clements' participation in the SMU scandal.

Channel 8 had already broken the story that SMU's athletic department continued to pay football players after the NCAA placed the school on probation. Still missing was proof that the payments had been authorized by someone higher up. *The News* was playing catchup on the story when Governor Clements asked to meet "chief executive to chief executive" with Burl Osborne. Clements admitted to Osborne that he and unspecified others had authorized the payments. But as a result of *The News'* delay in reporting the story, first Channel 8 and then the *Times Herald* broke it first. The ensuing scandal made national news. The NCAA banned football at SMU for a year, the first and only "death penalty" in the history of college football, and Osborne and *The News* were accused of attempting to protect a Republican governor.

The year was 1987, and three days before Osborne's meeting with the governor, Scott Bennett, an editorial writer at *The News*, received a phone call from a friend of his on Clements' staff. The governor wanted to talk about the SMU scandal, and hoped Osborne would lend a sympathetic ear. The governor's only condition was that no reporters be present.

By 1987, Osborne had left the newsroom to become president of *The News*, and it had been a long time since he covered a news event. He said he felt uncomfortable with the condition that there be no reporters present, but agreed to meet with the governor, and took editorial writer Scott Bennett with him.

The two flew to Austin and at their meeting with the governor, Clements began a long, rambling monologue. Soon it became apparent that he was implicating not just himself, but other unnamed SMU board members. Osborne began taping the conversation, but didn't press for names of these others. By the time Clements finished talking, there was scarcely time enough to catch the last plane home.

Arriving in Dallas at about 10:00 P.M., Osborne called his newsroom where, as had been arranged, Bill Evans was waiting for his call. Osborne told Evans what he had heard and added, as they both remember, that it was Evans' decision as to how the story should be handled. Evans said he didn't think it would be possible to get the story into the paper soon enough to reach more than a fraction of *The News*' readers. In any accusatory story *The News*' policy was (and is) to get a statement from all persons who could be adversely affected before the story runs. In this case, it meant calling SMU board members. Assuming they all could be reached, it meant the story wouldn't be ready to go into the paper until after midnight. Only readers in Dallas, and not all of them, would have it in their newspaper next morning. Since this was a story with state-wide implications, Evans elected to wait.

What neither he nor Osborne anticipated was that once Bennett returned to Dallas, he would call a friend and tell him about the meeting. Unfortunately, this friend also happened to be a friend of the news director at Channel 8. So the next morning, at the Governor's regularly scheduled press conference, a Channel 8 reporter knew enough to ask the right question. Clements admitted to having authorized the payments, and first Channel 8, and then the *Times Herald* broke the story.

Asked what he might have done differently, Osborne didn't half dodge the question, as he occasionally does when he wants to protect himself or others. He didn't say, "We didn't do anything wrong, and by God we'll never do it again." He said he would have insisted on taking a reporter along instead. A reporter would have asked more questions – and wouldn't have been as worried about missing the last flight home.

Until the *Times Herald* died, these various issues hadn't seemed to matter so much. But now they did, and would have to be dealt with.

Perpetual Motion

In the months following the death of the *Times Herald*, *The News* not only diversified its editorial pages, but dramatically broadened and deepened its news coverage. Needing new challenges to energize his newsroom, and fearful that Belo President Jim Sheehan wanted to raise profits by cutting costs, Osborne seized the initiative.

Sheehan had begun to talk about the need "to rationalize," and to ask whether "we can be all things to all people. We run more comic strips than any paper in the country," he said. "Fashion ! Dallas and the food section helped to get us where we are," but with the *Herald* gone, could some of these sections be combined? At one point, Sheehan even half-jokingly suggested that newsroom efficiency could be improved by keeping track of how many stories or column inches reporters contributed each week.

Osborne didn't listen. He was in no mood to slow down. He hadn't come to Dallas just to defeat the *Times*

Herald, but to create the extraordinary newspaper of distinction Robert Decherd had talked about.

So after Rick Connor, publisher of the *Fort Worth Star-Telegram,* accused Osborne of hypocrisy and warned *The News* to stay out of his home county, Osborne had a new enemy he could use to rally his troops. He beefed up news coverage and community sponsorships in Fort Worth, and tripled *The News'* circulation sales effort in the part of Tarrant county where most of the new homes were being built. He rode a helicopter over the area between the two cities and observed: "There appear to be no natural boundaries, no bunkers or forests or trenches that would stop us from advancing westward. Our surveys show that the new people moving in have interests and demographics closer to ours than to those of the *Star-Telegram.*"

Osborne didn't plan to launch an all-out assault on Fort Worth. With encouragement from Fort Worth's business leaders, *The News* had tried that earlier and failed – learning in the process that it is almost impossible to dislodge another newspaper in its home county. But he didn't back off either. "This time, it'll be more like cooking a frog. You drop him in a pot of boiling water and he'll jump right out. But if you put him into room temperature water, then slowly turn the heat up, he won't know until too late what hit him."

In February, as is his custom at the start of each year, Robert Decherd met with Osborne, Sheehan, and Pederson to discuss what positions *The News* should take on its editorial page in the months ahead. The meeting was a formality since it soon became apparent that most of the important decisions had already been made as part of the secret preparations for the *Herald's* demise.

Decherd quickly went down the list of topics Pederson had prepared, pausing to comment on only a few.

New police chief Bill Rathburn was off to a good start and certainly worth keeping around. *The News* would continue to advocate gun control, and urge that Dallas stop using the state's (unenforced) sodomy law as an excuse not to hire gay police officers. On the abortion issue, if the Supreme Court threw out Roe vs. Wade (which it later elected not to do), *The News* would favor the woman's right to choose during the first trimester, and abortions in the second trimester only to protect the life of the mother or in cases of rape or incest.

Decherd said *The News* must not support "willy-nilly" every well meaning project proposed by the city council, state legislature, or governor, but rather take greater care now to pick and choose. "Otherwise our support will become meaningless."

He asked about Pederson's position on bilingual education. She said, "we support it, but only as a bridge to early English proficiency, not as a permanent program." Pederson said that she was adding a second letters-to-the-editor feature, and a third page of commentary on Sundays. Carolyn Barta had polled readers on their preferences regarding columnists and the favorites were George Will, William Buckley, Mike Royko, and Georgie Ann Geyer (Will and Royko acquired from the *Times Herald*). These four would appear weekly, as would others less frequently: Ellen Goodman, David Broder, Lee Cullum, Michael Kingsley, and occasionally Mihkail Gorbachev. Two of *The News'* more conservative columnists, Bill Murchison and Richard Estrada, would be scaled back to once a week.

Osborne said that with so many columnists, Pederson would start running a few paragraphs from each on major issues. "It isn't often that a column contains more than two or three great paragraphs."

By April, four months after the *Herald's* demise, the newsroom had launched "Overnight," a daily entertainment page, and greatly expanded its Today section. The improvements were aimed at retaining former *Times Herald* readers, attracting working women, and at stemming whatever inroads the weekly *Dallas Observer* might be making among the young and restless.

Osborne said he got the idea for "Overnight" in November when, instead of watching the Mavericks lose their home opener to the Los Angeles Lakers, he and his teen-age son attended a Tom Petty concert at the Starplex auditorium. There, Osborne found himself surrounded by 17,000 foot-stomping, arm-waving, fifteen-to-thirty year olds, each an ideal candidate to become a lifetime *Morning News* reader. But then the next morning, although he found plenty in his newspaper about the Mavericks' loss, he couldn't find a single word about the concert.

Why not? Because the arts and entertainment section in which such a review should appear was printed a day in advance of the hard news sections. But also because entertainment reviewers were not accustomed to attending a rock concert, opera, or play, and then writing about it in an hour or less, the way sports writers have to do. Cultural events required thought and reflection, these reviewers said. Consequently entertainment reviews, whether high brow or low, seldom appeared in the paper until two or three days later. For popular events, *The News* often ran a preview story in advance of the concert instead.

Osborne was disturbed by this lack of urgency, this absence of freshness, when it came to covering events of such obvious interest to young people. But because he had been concerned with other things, or perhaps because given his background at AP he was more of a meat-and-potatoes, hard news kind of guy, he hadn't given it his attention until now. Decisions related to the soft side of the newspaper had usually been delegated to others.

Now this would change. The *Dallas Observer*, under new ownership, had in its Belo Watch column adopted what Osborne considered an "attack philosophy." *D* Magazine had stolen away Melissa Houtte, his former Sunday editor, and was upgrading its entertainment coverage. The *Times Herald*, considered by some the livelier of Dallas' two dailies, had closed its doors, and *The News'* ability to hold onto former *Herald* readers, Osborne now considered his greatest challenge.

Thus, by April 1, *The News* had grafted Overnight onto the back of its hard news metropolitan section. Overnight would have staffers enough so as many as five events could be reviewed from the night before. Halbreich spent half a million dollars promoting the new feature on radio and TV.

Also by April 1, the newsroom had expanded its Today section. Essays were out and lifestyle stories in. The Health and Fitness page was retained Monday, a Family section added Tuesday, a Woman section Wednesday, a Music page Thursday, an additional movie review Friday (four now instead of the previous three), and a film and video section Saturday. To enhance credibility of the Woman page, editors appointed an ethnically and otherwise diverse advisory panel of women.

To support Overnight and the expanded Today section, six new staffers were hired, including a country music critic. Dallas was the tenth largest radio market, but number one among country music listeners.

Two weeks later, *The News* won its fourth Pulitzer Prize – for the gritty "Abuse of Authority" series. The win represented a victory for the grunts and word people, and a rallying cry for reporters who had feared that with the *Herald* gone, their newspaper would become more cautious than ever. At the gala celebration, held at the Dallas Arboretum, Osborne took reporters Lorraine Adams and Dan Malone aside and told them to feel free to be as critical of him as they liked in their speeches. Both, however, chose to be gracious.

In the aftermath of the $58 million libel suit award against Belo's Channel 8 and the fallout from the South Texas case, editors had been assigning a higher priority to computer-assisted reporting. In an increasingly litigious society, they considered computer-assisted reporting to be less risky than relying on shoe leather and the occasional anonymous source.

Although there had been success stories – Olive Talley's prize-winning series on prison health abuse, and Bruce Tomaso's and Nancy Kruh's analysis showing which Dallas neighborhoods accounted for the most teen-age killings – most staffers still preferred traditional reporting methods instead.

In May, editors hired an editor from *USA Today* and an editor and veteran reporter from the *Wall Street Journal* to beef up their business coverage and create a new legal affairs beat. "We do a pretty good job of covering trials and confrontations," said Osborne. "What we haven't been covering is the process, the way justice fails to get dispensed in Texas. Too often justice is available only for those able to pay for it."

Business writers would now concentrate on writing more stories for page one, and on broadening their reach. Without "dumbing down" their approach, reporters would write less obviously for CEOs and board chairmen and more for the man on the street.

By the summer of 1992, at Robert Decherd's suggestion, the newsroom had created an urban affairs beat and a position for a Texas writer based in Dallas. Chris Kelley, the urban affairs writer, would go to Los Angeles and Sacramento to find out what mistakes California had made that Texas could learn from and avoid. Diane Jennings, the Texas writer, would look at the state in depth, then compare what she found with the situation in other large states with increasingly diverse populations.

Although Decherd and Osborne often talked about Belo buying other newspapers – *The Boston Globe* would be the ideal acquisition, they often said – Decherd's interests, like those of G. B. Dealey, his great-grandfather, seemed to be centered on Texas. If anything, he believed more strongly in positivism than before.

"The media can help us find problems before they become crises," he said in a recent speech. "But the media must also help us to find answers. Texans have only to look to neighboring states [Oklahoma and Louisiana] to appreciate the degree to which a negative or regressive press can cripple." Decherd insisted that *The News* not document problems without suggesting solutions as well.

"Once a city loses its optimism, once people begin to believe the possible to be impossible, a tremendous blow has been struck. People blame the media for creating conflict. But it's not the media that creates pettiness in the public arena. Pettiness is the creation of political opportunists, of people who understand that grandstanding inevitably attracts the attention of the press. We try not to promote opportunists.

"Texas' success has been a matter of natural resources, yes, but it's also been a mindset," he added in an interview. "A matter of who is going to set an agenda, who's willing to promote it, who's going to be relentless in holding the political sectors responsible.

"Why is Texas one of the most exciting places in the country today? Natural resources, D/FW and the services provided by Southwest Airlines, medical research and the medical centers and the billions of dollars they attract, and a welcoming environment for high technology that builds off the state's leadership in space and defense. These things didn't just happen because Texas had a lot of votes in Congress. They happened because we had a package that worked and a physical and geological setting to accommodate them. But if you go back to 1910, what was so different about Texas, Oklahoma, and Louisiana? Why us, and not them? I think a lot of things, but part of it was a positive press and I would submit to you that in this regard G. B. Dealey was at the head of the class."

Within six months of the *Times Herald's* demise, *The News* had disarmed many of its critics. But not all.

In the Spring of 1992, Ross Perot announced his candidacy for the presidency. *The News* had never been an unqualified Perot supporter. He was seen as too much of a maverick and self-promoter for that. But because Perot was from Dallas, Osborne wanted to ensure that *The News* applied the same meticulous standards to Perot's political campaign that it did to other sensitive local stories.

Thus, when Sam Attlesey broke the story that Perot's father had written President Johnson asking that Perot's son's Navy career be shortened, Osborne was upset. Sam had failed to mention that he'd gotten his information as part of a routine check at Johnson's presidential library in Austin. A reader might assume the story originated from the Bush or Clinton campaign headquarters. Osborne decreed that henceforth *The News* would refuse to investigate campaign tips unless the tipster agreed in advance that if the story was printed, his affiliation could be revealed.

The News looked into Perot's penchant for denying previously made statements. Reporters analyzed lawsuits filed against his company to show what they revealed about its personnel policies. And they discovered that Perot had published an article in which he said Texas schools were spending a "disproportionate amount of time" on the learning disabled rather than on people likely to become "future taxpayers." Perot sent word to Osborne that he thought his hometown paper "was being mean to him."

Osborne reacted by reading *all* of *The News'* election coverage with greater intensity. He searched for any examples of unfair reporting, however subtle, and he found some, not just in what was being said about Perot, but in coverage of the Bush and Clinton campaigns as well. He found paragraphs that started with the intrusive "however" or "in spite of," a story in which the reporter began several paragraphs with the judgmental "indeed," and still others in which opinion was stated as fact, as in: "Clinton prides himself on . . ." or "Perot was loath to. . . ." He found a story in which a reporter led with an unattributed quote.

He wondered if the people downstairs were trying to defy him. Ralph Langer, who normally mediates such disputes, was vacationing on the island of Maui at the time. So early one morning, Osborne went down to the third floor and angrily confronted *The News'* young political editor, a young man he hadn't met before. Word spread through the newsroom that their publisher was trying to protect Perot, and Belo Watch had a field day.

"I know it's nit-picky, but I can't help it," Osborne said later. "People are going to have to get used to it. I'm not going to change. Most of my complaints are about nuance or tone, a perception of bias, or the failure to present both sides of the argument.

"I'm finding more distrust of the political process, and of the news media, than at any time in my adult memory."

Contributing to the problem, he said, was the recent willingness of *The New York Times* to deviate from its page one philosophy of straightforward, factual reporting. The *Times*, by allowing Maureen Dowd to write front page essays that focused less on ideas and issues than on the personality quirks of the candidates, was offering an example that some writers at *The News* were tempted to imitate.

In July, when Perot suddenly dropped out of the race, there was the question of what sort of editorial to write. Rena Pederson wanted to say that Perot was a quitter, that he had let his supporters down big time. Osborne disagreed. He wasn't prepared to be so judgmental, and the two finally compromised.

"One of the most unfortunate aspects of Ross Perot's abrupt withdrawal from the race is that his long-promised package of issue positions, which was close to completion, will not receive the high-level debate it deserves," the editorial read. "Descriptions of the preliminary drafts reveal some daring, creative approaches to solving our nation's problems."

While a candidate, Perot refused to grant any interviews to *The Morning News*, electing to talk with members of the national press and national television media instead. After withdrawing from the race, he told Osborne he had expected his hometown newspaper to be more of a booster.

Six months after the *Times Herald* folded, research director Barbara Wells presented the results of a new Belden survey to company officers. Her findings showed that in picking up more than half the *Herald's* readers, *The News* had gained a disproportionate share of eighteen to twenty-four year olds, men, and African-Americans – but fewer women. The *Herald* had written more about the challenges women face in balancing work and family responsibilities and, according to Wells, apparently many working women had taken the occasion of the *Herald's* demise to stop taking a newspaper altogether. In this way, they could do so without feeling guilty. Apparently, too, the improvements *The News* recently had made in its Today and entertainment sections had yet to kick in.

But what made this new study unique, and laid the groundwork for future improvements, was that for the first time *The News* was in a position to measure the depth of loyalty readers felt for each section and feature. Wells had been able to obtain the names, addresses, and telephone numbers of all the people surveyed, and could go back and conduct follow-up interviews. Now if editors chose to cut back on the paper's three-and-a-half pages of comics or merge its Fashion ! Dallas and High Profile sections, for example, the decision could be made on a rational, rather than hit-or-miss, basis. And if an advertiser were to come in and say "I have only $20,000 to spend, and here are the kinds of customers I need to reach," *The News* could respond with facts as to which sections, and even which parts of sections, the advertiser could use to best effect. Loyalty as opposed to a mere frequency of readership measure is a more sophisticated approach.

In local politics, Diane Ragsdale, the African-American councilperson upset by Charlotte Mayes in the November City Council election, got enough signed petitions to force a recall election, the first in Dallas' history.

This time, although still endorsing Mayes – and calling Ragsdale mean-spirited and a poor loser – *The News* sent a reporter out to discover who Mayes' backers were. The story, published a month before the recall election, revealed that since Mayes' victory over Ragsdale, she had received $50,000 in new money from a star-studded list of white business leaders: oilman T. Boone Pickens, developer John M. Stemmons, and Dallas Mavericks owner Donald J. Carter, among others. By then, however, Ragsdale had self-destructed, refusing to campaign in the white parts of her district, or to talk with members of the white-controlled media.

Asked why *The News* failed to find out who Mayes' backers were before the November election, when it would have counted, metro editor Gilbert Bailon said that had a reporter proposed such a story then, it could have been interpreted as making a statement.

It was not long after the recall election that the City Council voted to cancel *The News'* contract to publish public notices, on grounds that there weren't enough minorities in upper management at either Belo or *The Morning News*.

SUMMING UP

"When you have to market your ideas,
you have to find more areas of commonalty."
– Richard Estrada

Two Years Later

When I revisited *The Morning News*
in August, 1994, at first I thought
little had changed except around the
edges.

The News still led the country in
total full-run and classified advertising, and now in retail full-run advertising as well. It still refused to accept personal dating ads. The street
price of the paper was still twenty-
five cents. And although the Sunday
price had been raised to $1.25 and
then $1.50, both daily and Sunday cir-
culation had continued to grow.

Women were still underrepre-
sented in newsroom management.
Burl Osborne still tossed firecrackers
into the newsroom in the form of
complaints about the importance of
nuance and tone. *Sports Illustrated*
had gigged *The News* for sending
thirty-two staffers to cover the Cowboys first Superbowl appearance since
1978, while having only one reporter
in Somalia at the time. The *Dallas
Observer's* Belo Watch still published

weekly critiques of the paper, though these had become shriller (a pro-file on Kroger's Dallas president was compared to a "long wet kiss," for example) and less accurate after Ralph Langer sent the staff a memo saying only he or Burl could answer questions from outsiders on policy matters.

Lori Stahl, now the Dallas-based political writer instead of backup city hall reporter, was still writing critically about Steve Bartlett:

"Dallas mayor Steve Bartlett, who pledged to restore order to City Hall, but drew fire for his 'Long Ranger' style, says he decided not to run again because he has almost finished the job. . . .

"Mr. Bartlett has been criticized by virtually every interest group in Dallas' contentious political theater: from business leaders and City Council members to minority residents and North Dallas voters he represented in some fashion for almost twenty years."

Robert Decherd was, if anything, more involved in helping to re-vitalize downtown through the Dallas Plan. He was also mobilizing business support to revitalize the one historically black college in North Texas, Paul Quinn, located in South Dallas.

Sports was still the only news department allowed to be irreverent.

"The Great Unwashed recall when Reunion Arena was praised as top of the line," Blackie Sherrod was writing. "The Great Unwashed may find it puzzling how such a structure could become so outmoded in a mere fifteen years, so that taxpayers must finance yet another downtown arena. The answer, of course, is that [basketball] Mavs and [hockey] Stars and Whoever demand a supply of luxury box suites now in vogue, where elite meet to sit and sip and pay through their bluenoses for the privilege."

Baseball writer Gerry Fraley was still trying to motivate the Texas Rangers.

"When [manager] John Oates walks into his new clubhouse, it will be culture shock. Baltimore was vanilla. The Rangers are Tutti Frutti. . . . To walk through the Rangers clubhouse is to take a stroll on the wild side. The mingling of Spanish and English-speaking players make the clubhouse an international bazaar . . . a loud, swirl-ing place full of peacock personalities given to flamboyance. . . .

How Oates handles the change will have a significant impact upon his standing as manager."

For the eleventh consecutive year, Dave Smith had won the Associated Press sports awards for best daily, best Sunday, and best special section.

The News had been slow to report that O. J. Simpson was a prime suspect in the murder of his ex-wife and her friend until doubly and triply sure the accusation was valid.

And although Belo President Jim Sheehan had retired at fifty-one, and executive managing editor Bill Evans at sixty-two – and neither been replaced – nearly everyone else seemed to be in the same job

It seemed as if little had changed, but appearances were deceiving.

In April, 1993, the Pulitzer board awarded its prize for spot news photography to Ken Geiger and William Snyder for their coverage of the summer Olympics. Photo editor John Davidson was finally named assistant managing editor for visuals, in belated recognition of the role photography and graphics have played in *The News'* success.

In April, 1994, *The News* won its sixth Pulitzer Prize for stories chronicling the universality of violence against women. Now, women in the newsroom said, male editors were showing a greater willingness to run tough stories about women's issues on page one. Thirty reporters, photographers, editors and graphic artists, led by international editor Jim Landers and his assistant international editor Patricia Gaston, put the series together. Gaston, reporters Gayle Reaves and Anne Reifenberg, and photographers Judy Walgren and Cindy Yamanaka, did much of the early brainstorming. The five photographers (Davidson insisted that they all be women) visited twelve countries on four continents. They documented abuses ranging from genital mutilation in Africa and rape as a national policy in Bosnia, to child prostitution in Thailand and sexual assaults by police officers in Dallas/Fort Worth.

Meanwhile, on the business side, Osborne and Halbreich had added three women and an African-American to the officer corps, and named an Hispanic to be advertising director. Among the new women officers was an Hispanic vice president of human resources.

Across the street, Robert Decherd had added an Hispanic and a second woman to Belo's board of directors. The Hispanic was Arturo Madero, the founding president of the Tomas Rivera Center, an institute for policy studies on Latino issues based in San Antonio, Texas, and Claremont, California. The woman, Dr. Judith Craven of Houston, was president of the United Way for the Texas gulf region.

In 1991, Dallas' Adelfa Callejo and former San Antonio mayor Henry Cisneros had invited Decherd to become a member of the board of the Tomas Rivera Center. By 1994, *The News* had dramatically increased its coverage of NAFTA, Mexico, and border issues. It had also stopped advocating that a wall be built at strategic points along the U.S./Mexico border.

In May of that year, the often critical *Columbia Journalism Review* praised *The News* for providing the most comprehensive coverage of border issues in the United States:

"In contrast to the one-person of the *Los Angeles Times*, *The Morning News* has bureaus in El Paso and Monterrey, as well as a business writer in its Austin bureau who focuses on international business, primarily Mexican business. . . .

"More than any other American paper, *The Morning News* has managed to integrate its Mexican and border news, particularly economic news, into its daily mix of stories."

In 1993, Mexico shipped $20 billion worth of goods to Texas, half the U.S. total. By 1994, thanks to the leadership of the Dallas business community–and *The Morning News*–Dallas, and not San Antonio or Houston, had become NAFTA's bridge city to Mexico. In editorials written by Timothy O'Leary (a former member of the NAFTA negotiating team), *The News* blasted Ross Perot for his opposition to NAFTA.

Meanwhile Richard Estrada, *The News'* point man on immigration issues, had mellowed some. In 1992, Senator Alan Simpson appointed Estrada to a bipartisan immigration reform commission chaired by former Texas congresswoman Barbara Jordan. There, Estrada says

The Dallas Morning News pressroom, 1963.
Courtesy A. H. Belo Archives.

9th victory points Cowboys toward the playoffs
Quarterback Steve Beuerlein leads late charge in 23-14 triumph over New Orleans
SPORTS, B-1

Dallas Times Herald

Today's paper for Dallas

★★★★

DECEMBER 9, 1991

©1991, Dallas Times Herald

25 CENTS

MONDAY

GOODBYE, DALLAS!

Tears, toasts, hugs and handshakes as last edition marks end of paper's 112 years of journalism history

Newspaper's staff mourns loss of friend

By Mark Potok
OF THE TIMES HERALD STAFF

At first, as Dallas Times Herald staffers picked up their telephones on a gray and drizzly Sunday morning, it felt like a punch to the solar plexus. Then came shock, a kind of numbness, desperation at the economic implications. In the end, there was merely sadness.

The newspaper they loved was dead.

"This was like a dream," said a weeping Dennis Whitaker, 41, who began work as assistant metro editor on the 112-year-old newspaper just one week ago today. "This was home. This was a good newspaper. This was good journalists, and professional people.

"My head feels like it's going to blow up."

From one end of the downtown Dallas newspaper building to the other, staffers gathered in knots, talking, crying, occasionally speaking in angry tones of the passing of an old friend. As they drifted in, walking past newly hired security guards, they embraced old friends, people they'd worked with for years, even colleagues they'd never talked to before.

And even then, they spoke of their readers.

"My greatest regret is I did not get the opportunity to say goodbye to all the people who read me for 40 years," said Bob Brock, broadcast editor and the longest-serving editorial employee in the building. "These people have been very precious to me. It is readers that make a newspaper. It is not writers."

Added William A. Scott, who covered City Hall for the Times Herald: "Unfortunately, Dallas, the eighth-largest city in America, will only be left with one newspaper.

"It's a sad day for everyone."

Metro Editor Nancy Laughlin was one of those who had to call staff members after learning the news Sunday morning. "One person laughed hysterically," she said. "One person cried hysterically." For most people, it was just this stunned

Please see STAFF, A-11

Printer Phil Grant, right, pastes up today's lead headline as Editor Roy E. Bode, left, and makeup editor Jerry A. McNeill watch.

Steve Arkows/Dallas Times Herald

Recession took its toll on paper

By Jim Henderson
OF THE TIMES HERALD STAFF

One hundred and twelve years after it began on a hand-fed press hauled to town on an ox cart, the Dallas Times Herald ceased publication today.

"The action was inevitable," said Publisher John Buzzetta, in
■ Readers share their stories of losing an old friend. **Page A-11**
■ Molly Ivins: Times Herald had the writers, the guts. **A-11**
■ Skip Bayless: The war is over, and we all lose. **Page B-1**
announcing that substantially all of the paper's assets had been sold to the rival Dallas Morning News for $55 million.

The recession has been especially difficult for media companies and particularly hard on the second newspaper company in a market. There was just not enough revenue in this marketplace for us to make it. We've been in a national recession for two years and a regional recession since 1985.

Buzzetta said that during the past year he had approached "more than 100 potential investors or buyers for the newspaper" in an attempt to keep it alive. However, he said, "these efforts were unsuccessful."

He said the company does not anticipate filing bankruptcy and expects to pay all of its suppliers. All 900 employees will receive salary and benefits for at least 60 days, Buzzetta said.

Times Herald employees began receiving the word early on a gray Sunday morning. Although negotiations with The Morning News had been ongoing for two months, most workers were not aware that the paper's demise was imminent.

Please see CLOSE, A-10

Briefly...

- **EX-HOSTAGE GETS OK TO LEAVE HOSPITAL**/A-3
- **YELTSIN UNVEILS PLAN FOR A NEW UNION**/A-5
- **GOLF COURSE TRAGEDY TOOK CASH, LIVES**/A-15

IN LIFESTYLE
- **MAGAZINE PUTS BLACK FOCUS ON TEXAS**/D-1

LAST CANDLE LIGHTED
Israelis at Mideast peace talks in Washington light Hanukkah candles Sunday. From left are Yosef Ben-Aharon, Uri Lubrani and Elyakim Rubinstein.

The Associated Press

INSIDE
STEVE SMITH: Jessica Tandy and hints of "Miracle on 34th Street" can't redeem the ending of "The Story Lady," but there's still plenty to recommend it.
PAGE D-1

BUSINESS	D-1	MOVIES	D-4,7
COMICS	D-6,8	OBITUARIES	A-16
DALLAS/TEXAS	A-15	SPORTS	B-1
DR. BROTHERS	D-2	TV LISTINGS	D-8
EDITORIALS	A-18	WEATHER	A-17

Home Delivery 343-7253
Classified 748-1414

Thank you, Dallas!

We were part of your life for 112 years. You supported us loyally, helping us achieve distinction as one of America's leading newspapers.

Dallas is fortunate in that it fostered two great newspapers, so one paper of great quality will remain tomorrow.

Our regret is that we no longer will be a guest in your home, a faithful companion.

You were great company. And it was a wonderful life!

John Buzzetta, Publisher
Roy E. Bode, Editor
and every employee of the
Dallas Times Herald

Front page of last day's edition of the *Dallas Times Herald*.

The Dallas Morning News

Texas' Leading Newspaper   © 1991, The Dallas Morning News   Dallas, Texas, Monday, December 9, 1991   6 Sections   B   • • •   25 Cents

Times Herald shuts down today

Owner of News buys assets for $55 million

By Richard Alm and Bruce Tomaso
Staff Writers of The Dallas Morning News

TIMES HERALD CLOSES AFTER 112 YEARS

- Buzzetta resolute.   17A
- Times Herald history.   18A
- The News' history.   18A
- How employees got word.   19A
- Recession hurt paper.   19A
- How deal happened.   21A
- Some answers about deal.   21A
- Decherd statement.   21A
- Readers, advertisers note.   21A
- Editorial.   22A

Dallas Times Herald page makeup editor Jerry McNeill puts down the top front-page headline Sunday as the news-paper's final edition is prepared for delivery Monday. Mr. McNeill worked at the Times Herald for 18 years.

PURCHASE TERMS
Acquisition of assets from Times Herald Printing Co.

Closing of newspaper mourned across Dallas

By Lee Hancock
Staff Writer of The Dallas Morning News

Key Soviet republics form new alliance

Action dooms Gorbachev's push to save union

By George Rodrigue
European Bureau of The Dallas Morning News

- Republics at a glance.   7A

Dentist-infected AIDS patient dies

Case prompted debate on testing

New York Times News Service

Suspect arrested in slayings of 4

Golf course employee accused in 'brutal' killings of colleagues

By Nancy St. Pierre
Staff Writer of The Dallas Morning News

- Profile of victims.   6A

Cowboys defeat Saints, 23-14

Cowboys wide receiver Michael Irvin exults Sunday as Dallas beats New Orleans. He set a Dallas record for catches in a season with 78. (Story on Page 1B.)

Democrats strive to tap middle-class frustration in '92

By Susan Feeney
Washington Bureau of The Dallas Morning News

INSIDE
Sports downtown

Dallas-Fort Worth area — Mostly cloudy with a chance of showers.
More weather on Page 8D.

Kent State remembered
Page 25A and Page 1G

It's a filly at the Derby
Genuine Risk wins, Page 1B

The saga of silver and the Hunts
Pages 8-9A

The Dallas Morning News
sunday
Morning Final

Texas' leading newspaper ★★★★□   Dallas, Texas, Sunday, May 4, 1980   Price 50 Cents

Bush stems Reagan momentum

Sheriff's primary winner Don Byrd kisses his wife amid GOP landslide.

ELECTIONS AT A GLANCE

As of 12:00 a.m.

PRESIDENT
DEMOCRATIC
(Statewide)

	Popular vote	Pct.
Jimmy Carter	566,540	56
Ted Kennedy	228,909	22
Jerry Brown	26,864	3
Uncommitted	200,577	19

(Countywide)

Jimmy Carter	35,425	66.39
Ted Kennedy	12,226	22.91
Jerry Brown	1,090	2.04
Uncommitted	4,516	8.65

REPUBLICAN
(Statewide)

Ronald Reagan	217,130	52
George Bush	196,662	47
Uncommitted	6,191	1

(Countywide)

Ronald Reagan	16,100	51.95
George Bush	14,328	45.97
Uncommitted	644	2.06

REPUBLICAN DELEGATES

Ronald Reagan	58
George Bush	22
Uncommitted	0

SHERIFF
DEMOCRATIC

Lou Acker	7,565
Bob Collins	10,522
Ralph Yarborough	5,535
Al Maddox	13,330
Chuck Ryan	1,264
Bill Dear	4,724

REPUBLICAN

| Carl Thomas | 5,570 |
| Don Byrd | 23,221 |

RAILROAD COMMISSION
(Statewide)
Full term
DEMOCRATIC

| John Poerner | 273,085 |
| Buddy Temple | 333,238 |

REPUBLICAN

Henry Grover	35,685
John T. Henderson	19,768
E.W. (Billy) Kidd	12,545

Unexpired term
DEMOCRATIC

| Jim Hightower | 264,358 |
| Jim Nugent | 315,742 |

GOP REFERENDUM
(Statewide)
Wiretapping in drug cases

| In favor 55,100 | Against 11,137 |

Initiative and Referendum

| In favor 58,450 | Against 7,875 |

(Countywide)
Wiretapping in drug cases

| In favor 10,720 | Against 2,779 |

Initiative and Referendum

| In favor 11,659 | Against 1,725 |

Beauty contest goes to Carter

By CAROLYN BARTA
Political Editor of The News

Texan George Bush garnered a stunning percentage of the statewide popular vote in Texas' Republican presidential primary Saturday while picking up more than a third of the 80 GOP delegates.

President Carter whipped Sen. Edward Kennedy in the Democratic primary "beauty contest" but "uncommitted" voters drew almost as many votes as Kennedy, indicating a visible rejection of both major candidates.

Initial indications from the 4,000 precinct conventions where the selection process for Texas' 152 Democratic delegates began was that Kennedy won less than one-third of the delegates in the first of three convention rounds which ends at the state convention June 20-21.

As late as two weeks ago, Reagan campaign predictions were that Bush would get nine to a maximum of 12 delegates in his home state, but after his Pennsylvania primary win, Bush national campaign manager Jim Baker was hoping for one-third of the Texas delegation.

The lead increased early between

See LATE on Page 7A.

INSIDE ON ELECTIONS

State Rep. Buddy Temple takes a lead in railroad commission race, Page 16A.

Former State Sen. Ralph Hall apparently wins Democratic primary in 4th Congressional District, Page 16A.

Carter claims 2-to-1 victory in delegates, Page 55A.

Reagan and Bush, with the New England duo adopted Texas pening the former California governor mainly on the basis of large early returns from the Houston area.

Reagan steadily inched ahead in votes from the conservative, rural areas were tabulated. Statewide totals at 11 p.m. showed Reagan with 51 percent of the vote to Bush's 46 percent and one percent uncommitted, with 45 percent of the precincts reporting. Carter was winning 56 percent of

See LATE on Page 7A.

Byrd puts Thomas away
Sheriff's aide blames 'deal with Democrats'

By SAM ATTLESEY
Political Writer of The News

Soon after his stunning upset in 1976, Sheriff Carl Thomas proclaimed that he wanted to be Dallas County sheriff for 40 years.

A record number of voters went to the Republican primary Saturday to tell Thomas four years was plenty, thank you.

Less than a year after Thomas had been in office, the rumors started that Dallas Police Chief Don Byrd was interested in running for the office.

And 80 percent of that record turnout — which apparently recorded many independents and Democrats — cast their votes for Byrd, who campaigned on the theme of "law and order."

Byrd's victory was no real surprise to most observers. But the wide margin of his victory shocked even supporters of the former police chief.

The 52-year-old Byrd was the beneficiary of much of the issue of a massive crossover vote of Independents and conservative Democrats, which resulted in the record turnout.

Lynn Burk, Thomas' chief deputy and close ally, blamed the loss on a collaboration between the Democratic Party and the business establishment.

"We think there was a deal made with the Democrats to make Don Byrd to cross over to the Republican Party so that he could defeat Sheriff Thomas," Burk said.

Even in defeat, Thomas was controversial, speaking out of his campaign headquarters and leaving about 75 supporters wondering where he had gone.

Where he had gone was to a private party at a Northeast Dallas motel, where he met with family members and a select group of deputies.

Thomas granted interviews to only one television station and one radio station. In those interviews he reportedly said, "Now I can treat people the way I want ... now I can live like a normal human being."

Although virtually all of the attention was on the GOP battle, a half dozen candidates were battling in the Democratic primary.

That apparently will result in a runoff between two former sheriff's deputies, both of whom had been fired by Thomas.

In fact, Bob Collins, the leading Democratic votegrabber had been fired twice by Thomas.

Collins apparently will face another former deputy, Al Maddox, who had sought the sheriff's post in 1976.

Collins, a 49-year-old former Marine Corps drill instructor, and the silver-haired Maddox, 49, 13-year veteran of the sheriff's office, were the two front-runners.

Will growth pains stunt N. Dallas?

By HENRY TATUM

The words "growth" and "Dallas" have been interchangeable for as long as many people can remember.

But the phenomenal development of Far North Dallas, accompanied by less-than-adequate roads, has prompted some city officials to consider imposing an era of no growth on its northern fringe.

The first traces of the program are being drawn.

Officials have called a halt to new zoning in the area until a master plan can be prepared to deal with the massive traffic problems that rapid growth has created.

Although growth constrictions

are being contemplated for Far North Dallas, one city councilman wants to encourage more development in the southern half of the city.

The construction boom north of LBJ Freeway, in a section that real estate brokers have dubbed the "Golden Corridor," already has prompted estimates that now

See SOUTHERN on Page 16A.

Index

Books	44G	Horoscope	31
Business	No. E	Line 1	38A
Classified	26-41D	Movies	No. C
Crossword	44A	Obituaries	48A
Editorials	31	Real Estate	4F
Energy	12K	Scrabble-Grams	4AA
Entertainment	Sec. C	Television	1V-Tab
Financial	4-14H	Texas & Tour	14A
Getting Along	7AA	Travel	Sec. J
Headlines	6AA	Viewpoints	3G

Weather

Dallas-Fort Worth area — Partly cloudy through Monday. Highs Sunday and Monday in the upper 70s. Low Sunday in the mid-50s. Saturday's high: 76.

Weather on Page 29A.

2 released

Gunmen occupying the Iranian embassy in London release two more hostages, Page 11I.

Alien tide swamps U.S. Border Patrol

By HOWARD SWINDLE and GEORGE KUEMPEL
Staff Writers of The News

LAREDO, Texas — The shadows had turned to darkness, and the silent invasion across the winding Rio Grande already was under way.

A squelch, then a message, on the 2-way radio pierced the silence as the two border patrolmen set in their 4-wheel-drive Ramcharger amid the thick chinota that almost shields the sight of the river 15 feet to their left.

A whine crackling over the radio told them a smuggler, a "coyote," had backed a bajo semitrailer into a hiding place along the murky river and was loading 150 illegal Mexican aliens aboard.

That's the same place where they

loaded 150 wetbacks earlier today."

But, anticlimactically, there was no rush to arrest the smuggler and his load of human cargo.

The two border patrolmen, like their 46 or so colleagues who work out of the Laredo headquarters, didn't have enough gasoline.

"Three miles outside the city limits — and we haven't got enough gas to go out and get them," Cogburn said bitterly. "If you load 500 in an open truck and drive just on the outside of the city limits, we'd have to wave at you."

The message had come down from Washington only a few days earlier — stop the 500,000 or more Mexican aliens who slip illegally into the United States every year, but don't use any gasoline. There's been a budget cut.

Gasoline was rationed to three gallons

See PATROLMEN on Page 18A.

Illegal aliens climb out of a rail car after a search by border patrolmen.

The Dallas Morning News

Texas' Leading Newspaper   © 1993, The Dallas Morning News   Dallas, Texas, Wednesday, February 10, 1993   13 Sections   HFGM   ••••   25 Cents

300,000 jam rally for Cowboys

26 in police custody, at least 21 hurt in scattered violence

Dallas police form a protective circle around fellow officers as they restrain two people at Commerce and Griffin streets Tuesday amid violence at the Dallas Cowboys Super Bowl parade. Several bottles were thrown at the officers as they scuffled with the paradegoers.

Two Dallas Cowboys fans stand on a traffic signal pole Tuesday as a blizzard of confetti drops on the Super Bowl championship parade on Commerce Street. Officials estimated that more than 300,000 people crowded downtown to view the players, coaches and bands.

Exuberant fans embrace NFL champs

By Jeffrey Weiss
Staff Writer of The Dallas Morning News

The best of the Dallas Cowboys' Super Bowl celebration Tuesday was unbridled silver-and-blue exuberance. The worst was vicious, destructive violence.

City officials estimated that more than 300,000 people packed downtown for more than two hours. Dallas Area Rapid Transit officials said their free bus service transported about 19,000 more people downtown than on a normal day, spokesman Ron Whittington said. The crowd was swelled by thousands of students who ignored an edict that they stay in school.

Tuesday's celebration, including a ticker-tape parade and a ceremony at City Hall Plaza, was the biggest event that downtown Dallas had ever hosted. It also was poorly controlled, city officials acknowledged.

Most of the thousands who went downtown left happy. But sporadic fighting tainted the revelry, sending at least 21 people to hospitals, including a toddler. Police arrested 16 adults and detained 10 juveniles.

The most seriously injured person, a 44-year-old man, was in serious condition at Methodist Medical.

Please see 300,000 PACK on Page 27A.

Teen groups terrorize bystanders

Fans attacked, businesses looted, buses vandalized

By Al Brumley
Staff Writer of The Dallas Morning News

Swarms of teen-agers tore through downtown Dallas after Tuesday's parade honoring the Cowboys, overwhelming police and terrorizing bystanders in the worst unrest in recent city history.

Police attributed the violence to "overexuberance" on the part of Cowboys fans, but it was clear that many youths were using race and gang loyalties as reasons to attack.

"There's black people jumping on white people, and that just ain't right," said 18-year-old Yolanda Haggard, a black teen-ager who frantically sought cover during the melee.

"They're just throwing bottles and hitting each other for nothing. I'm scared to walk to my bus stop. They're just fighting here for nothing. It don't make sense."

Trouble surfaced more than an hour before the parade's start with reports of cars being rocked and racial tensions already escalating. The outright violence erupted at

Please see TEEN-AGERS on Page 25A.

Rathburn says he ordered force strengthened on eve of parade

Miscalculation left city vulnerable to mayhem, many officers say

By Todd Copilevitz
and Ed Housewright
Staff Writers of The Dallas Morning News

On the eve of the Dallas Cowboys' Super Bowl parade, Police Chief Bill Rathburn ordered the head of the event's security to nearly double the number of officers assigned because he considered the existing plans inadequate, the chief said Tuesday night.

But even after the chief issued the order to Deputy Chief Granvel Tolliver to call in an additional 120 officers, police did not consider violence likely, nor did they anticipate that the crowd would be so enormous, Chief Rathburn said.

"It was my sense and the sense of others that violence wouldn't be a problem," the chief said late Tuesday after returning from a day trip to Atlanta. "Obviously we misjudged it."

INSIDE
- Racial undercurrents. 22A
- A look at victims. 25A
- Chronology of events. 25A
- Photo page. 26A
- Students play hooky. 27A
- Fan goes into labor. 27A
- Other cities' experiences. .. 28A

That miscalculation, coupled with miscues throughout the day Tuesday, left the city vulnerable to the melee that ensued downtown, many street officers and supervisors said.

They pointed out that Chief Tolliver, who was in charge of the Police Department's security measures, was in the parade. Often, calls to the deputy chief on police radios went unanswered.

Please see RATHBURN on Page 24A.

Clinton cutting quarter of staff in White House reorganization

By Kathy Lewis
Washington Bureau of The Dallas Morning News

WASHINGTON — Moving to make good on a campaign promise, President Clinton ordered a 25 percent cut in staff Tuesday as he reorganized the White House and defined the federal government's duties to more with less.

"In government cannot ask other American people to change if American people to change if I don't do the same," he said. "I want a leaner staff that not only works better but would work better."

He often, in recent years, our economy had been on automatic

Glance at cutbacks 10A

pilot. People do things today just because that's the way they were done yesterday," he said.

Government, he said, has grown to satisfy "not only the needs of the people, but its own needs."

The next cuts are expected to come Wednesday, when the president orders agencies to trim administrative costs by 3 percent and cancels some perks traditionally given top officials.

Making cuts described by aides as both symbolic and real, Mr. Clinton

Please see CLINTON on Page 10A.

INSIDE
GOP plan for race

Texas Republican leaders circulate a memo that questions the integrity of Democratic candidates in the special U.S. Senate election.
Page 40A.

Area Leaders	3C
Metropolitan	
Business	1-11D
National	1-3AA
Classified	Sec. G
Movies	4C
Comics	13-15C
National	4-8A
Crossword	13-14C
	21-12A
Dear Abby	13C
Obituaries	36A
Editorials	30A
Overnight	36A
Fashion/Dallas	1C
Sports	Sec. B
	Sec. E
Television	7C
Food	Sec. F
Texas & Sweet	
Horoscope	13C
	40A, 41C
International	
Today	Sec. C
	16A, 18A, 20A
Viewpoints	31A
Weather on Page 24A

Ruling clouds Arlington plant's future

Judge orders GM to drop plans to consolidate Willow Run facility

By Richard A. Oppel Jr.
Staff Writer of The Dallas Morning News

A Michigan state judge on Tuesday ordered General Motors to drop plans to close its Willow Run plant and move production to Arlington, clouding once again the future of both plants.

Although the unusual court decision won't have any immediate effect on Arlington, the long-range effect is unclear.

As part of a plan to cut 74,000 jobs by 1995, the No. 1 automaker said last year that it would shut down its operations at Willow Run, near Ypsilanti, Mich., by July and move

Comparison of plants 9A
Employee reaction 1D

some workers to Arlington, where more than 3,500 people are employed.

GM officials said they will seek an expedited appeal of the ruling. They said they have no contingency plans if the appeals courts say GM must keep Willow Run open, but they also said they believe that there is virtually no chance that would occur.

The company declined to speculate on whether Arlington would be affected if Tuesday's ruling were

Please see RULING on Page 9A.

upheld. "We consider it so hypothetical that we haven't even thought about that happening," said Lee Schotman, a GM lawyer.

"We feel that if we get proper consideration in the appellate courts, this ought to be a very easy decision to overturn. This has never happened anywhere, and the judge knows that.

The ruling against GM on Tuesday was yet another setback to the company, which is scrambling to defend the safety of millions of its pickup trucks and is expected Thursday to announce a closing

Please see RULING on Page 9A.

This front page from 1993 shows how the format has changed and how *The Morning News* takes care to balance good news and bad.

The Dallas Morning News president and general manager, Jeremy Halbreich.
The Dallas Morning News file photo.

Belo Chairman and CEO Robert Decherd, 1992. Photo by William Snyder.

Ben Decherd, 1970.
Photo by Gittings.

Burl Osborne (center) making a point at the 10 o'clock meeting.
To his right is vice president and controller Barry Peckham, to his left is information
management vice president, Grover Livingston.
Photo by Cindy Yamanaka.

Rena Pederson (center) meeting with members of her editorial board.
From left to right: Carolyn Barta, Henry Tatum, Pederson, Richard Estrada,
and Jesse James. Photo by Kent Barker.

Lorraine Adams and Dan Malone celebrating their win of the
1992 Pulitzer Prize for investigative reporting for their series
"Abuse of Authority."
The Dallas Morning News file photo.

Bob Mong (left) and newsroom employees share a homemade video roasting Stuart Wilk (seated). Columnist Maryln Schwartz is behind Wilk. Texas and the Southwest editor Donnis Baggett (now assistant managing editor in charge of the Sunday product) is at right. *The Dallas Morning News* file photo.

(left to right) Bill Evans, Ralph Langer, photo editor
John Davidson (standing), and photographer David Woo
deciding which pictures to use in coverage of crash of
Delta flight 191 (1985). *The Dallas Morning News* file photo.

Photo by Ken Geiger showing winning hands of American swimmer
Pablo Morales, from series with William Snyder that won 1993 Pulitzer Prize
for spot news photography of coverage of 1992 summer olympics.

Photo by Ken Geiger showing Nigerian women celebrating
their win of bronze medal, from series with William Snyder that won
1993 Pulitzer Prize for spot news photography for coverage of
1992 summer olympics.

A Somali girl awaits her turn to be circumcised.
From the 1994 Pulitzer Prize winning series on violence against women.
Photo by Judy Walgren.

he found that "when you have to market your ide
more areas of commonalty."

He learned that "Los Angeles County has more
the whole state of Texas," and that given Texas
twinned cities along the Rio Grande, there are closer
ties among Mexicans and Mexican-Americans than
where very different conditions prevail.

In November, 1991, *The News* urged voters not to s
issue aimed at improving the condition of *colonias* alo
Mexico border. By the summer of 1994, *The News* was
editorial:

"Thirty years ago, Appalachia was the most powerful
poverty in America. Today the rural ghettos of the Texas-M
der have assumed that dubious distinction. The entire nati
stake in how the issue of the *colonias* is handled."

The barriers between a once aggressively conservative e
page and a moderate newsroom were coming down.

Whether by accident or by design, Belo's Channel 8 has had a
image among Mexican-Americans than *The Morning News*. Per
this was because Channel 8 is run mostly by Texans; *The News* u
Decherd and Osborne by people from elsewhere. Or perhaps it
because Channel 8 prides itself on doing whatever it does "in the spi
of Texas," while *The News* sometimes seemed more concerned wit
not getting beat by the *New York Times* or *Wall Street Journal* on
Texas story.

But now there appeared to be a shift. Diane Jennings, the new
"Texas writer," was writing story after story about what makes
today's Texas unique.

"Authors write about it. Businesses commercialize it. Country-
Western singers croon about it.

"But Texans simply feel it—a sense of belonging to a certain spot
between the Red River and the Rio Grande.

"They can't explain it, but like the hot winds of a Texas summer,
they know it's there.

". . . . According to a 1993 Texas poll, more than sixty per cent of

people believe that Texans are different from the rest of the world. Evidence of that feeling pervades the state, from the ubiquitous Lone Star flag to the 'Don't Mess with Texas' anti-letter campaign.

" . . . . That 'state of mind' has survived political, social and economic upheaval, but whether it flourishes in the future is debatable.

" . . . . The ethnic makeup of Texas is shifting. By 2026, Texas is expected to have a 'majority minority' population. Though today's ethnic Texans have developed a unique sense of place, it has been in spite of the legends that personify Texas. Traditionally, the victory-or-death Alamo defenders and their rugged, self-reliant cowboy have been portrayed as white."

Since I'd seen him last, Osborne had been named chairman of the American Press Institute, president of the Texas Daily Newspaper Association, and a member of the board of directors of the Associated Press. In a sense, he was now the boss of his old boss, Lou Boccardi, at AP.

Robert Decherd was now chairman of the public policy committee of the Newspaper Association of America and had agreed to move up through the chairs, eventually to become its president.

By the end of 1994, *The News* ranked third (after the *Chicago Tribune* and *Philadelphia Inquirer*) in number of stories (nearly 6000) placed in papers that subscribe to the Knight-Ridder/Tribune news service. More significant than the quantity was the fact the stories placed were no longer predominantly in sports or business, but increasingly entertainment and lifestyle features as well.

In May, 1993, Susan Decker, an analyst with the Wall Street firm of Donaldson, Lufkin & Jenrette, published a comparison of the Dallas and Boston newspaper markets in which she criticized *The News* for failure to take advantage of its profit potential.

"*The Morning News* maintains significantly lower advertising and circulation rates than the *Boston Globe*. Certainly this is partly a vestige of aggressive competition with the *Times Herald* until it closed in December of 1991. Yet a year and a half later, CPMs [the cost per

thousand of advertising linage] are even lower than when the *Herald* was operational. With the other natural advantages of the Dallas market, minimal unionization, no other daily Dallas newspapers . . . the margin potential of *The Morning* News is phenomenal under more aggressive pricing conditions.

"We think *The Morning News* can generate consistently higher margins than very profitable papers like the *San Jose Mercury News* or *The Commercial Appeal* in Memphis . . . comforting news in an industry that . . . appears to be mired in a several year period of modest growth."

At Belo, Susan Decker's analysis was ignored.

In *The News'* response, Jeremy Halbreich said, "We can justify having lower absolute ad rates since our cost of doing business is lower than the *Globe's* and we believe that we buy newsprint more efficiently as well."

In September, 1993, Belo president Jim Sheehan, who had been known to favor a more aggressive pricing policy, retired, saying he needed to spend more time with his family. A year earlier, Sheehan's daughter had been killed in a freak automobile accident, and in the Spring of 1993 the hoped-for acquisition of the *Boston Globe* had fallen through when *The New York Times* company bought the paper instead. For the foreseeable future, there didn't appear to be many other corporate challenges on the horizon.

Decherd, in announcing Sheehan's retirement, said Jim's contributions had been "legion," particularly with respect to establishing Belo's credibility in the investment community, and in strategic initiatives. Decherd added the title of president to his other titles of chairman and chief executive officer, and eliminated the position of chief operating officer. Osborne now reported directly to Decherd again, as he had prior to 1987 when Sheehan was named president and chief operating officer.

At *The News*, Osborne began delegating more authority to Langer, Halbreich, and Pederson, and spending more time with Decherd across the street. Soon, Belo had helped form a consortium of newspaper companies that included Central Newspapers of Indianapolis;

Cowles Media Company of Minneapolis; Freedom Communications of Irvine, California; McClatchy Newspapers of Sacramento, California; and Pulitzer Publishing Company of St. Louis. The goal was to research the use of technology for new products.

Now, Osborne was predicting that *The News* would become the franchise for information about the Dallas Cowboys and NAFTA, information that anyone in the country (or Mexico) could access electronically. He was working with Ralph Langer to launch a weekly religion section which he expected to become still another franchise. He predicted that since telephone companies were being allowed to team up with cable television companies, the day should soon come when newspapers and network television stations owned by the same company in the same market would be allowed to work together as well. When that happened, reporters and editors at both *The News* and Channel 8 would be challenged to develop a whole new set of skills.

And both he and Robert Decherd emphasized that they still hoped to acquire one or more newspapers in the 50,000 to 250,000 circulation range. Independent, family-owned or controlled papers in Columbus, Minneapolis, Milwaukee, San Diego, and Providence, all looked attractive, said Osborne. But none were available.

By late 1994, Osborne agreed to fold *Dallas Life, The News'* locally produced magazine. It was losing two million dollars a year. By letting it die, he would have money for improvements in other parts of the paper. The photographers who had used *Dallas Life* as a showcase for their work would be given additional space in the "A" section of the paper. Writers like Bill Minutaglio and Bryan Woolley who had done their best work for *Dallas Life* would be encouraged to write for page one now instead. Osborne was willing to be more flexible now.

"Burl's an intense guy," said Ralph Langer. "He has lots of highs and lows. He has fewer lows now that he reports directly to Robert again."

"It's like walking up a down escalator; you can't stand still, you've got to keep moving. If you don't keep improving, you wind up with decline or decay."
– Burl Osborne, October, 1994

"It will be a tragedy if we don't transform ourselves as much in the next ten years as we have the past ten." – Bob Mong

Conclusions

Futurists have called newspapers the last of the great smokestack industries – decrepit, dated, and destined to die. I hope this book offers proof, if proof is needed, that this need not be so.

In recent months there has been a spate of stories in the *New York Times* and elsewhere about the need for journalists to stop being so cynical, and about news becoming the enemy of hope.

"The notion that cynicism has replaced a necessary skepticism as the core of American journalism may be supplanting the more traditional criticism that coverage is warped by ideological (usually liberal) bias," wrote William Glaberson in the *Times*. "Many critics now worry about a politically neutral bias that shapes news coverage by declaring that all public figures, indeed all people in the news, are suspect. In this version of journalism, all politicians are manipulative, all business people are venal and all proposals have ulterior motives."

A nation-wide Yankelovich survey showed that fifty per cent of the people interviewed in 1988 said they had a great deal of confidence in news from newspapers, but by 1993, that number had dropped to twenty per cent.

The Dallas market may be unique. The virtually union-free *Morning News* may be able to operate more economically than other papers its size. But in its emphasis on credibility, civility, and community involvement – and in its leaders' willingness to learn from past mistakes – *The News* could well be offering a model for other papers to follow. Its cooler, more neutral style of reporting seems more palatable than a journalism of advocacy these days. Many Americans appear to be fed up with a news media that tells them how to think.

Fifteen years ago, Steve Star, a professor at the Harvard Business School, conducted a series of seminars under the auspices of the American Newspaper Publishers Association. Owners, editors, and general managers were challenged to disprove assumptions suggesting that if newspapers didn't change, their days were numbered. The assumptions were:

– That newspapers have passed from being a necessary product to a discretionary one. Too often they are thought of as a commodity, like sugar, with one brand indistinguishable from another, rather than a performance product that people have to have.

– That a newspaper's great strength is habit, and the frailty of that strength becomes all too apparent in times of escalating circulation prices.

– That at most newspapers, editorial, advertising, circulation, and promotion departments operate as separate fiefdoms with little coordination of objectives. Publishers seldom act as marketing strategists.

– And that the approach of providing a cafeteria of information, of trying to be all things to all people, must be examined in terms of building on unique strengths. Cafeterias are losing business to the fast food industry. General purpose magazines are dying.

In winning the great Texas newspaper war – and in the years since – *The Morning News* has successfully challenged all these assumptions. As other public companies concerned themselves with quarterly earnings improvement, bought cable TV stations, or diversified into electronic information services, *The News* took a different approach.

What has made *The Morning News* unique – and has contributed immeasurably to its success – has been its owners' willingness to be satisfied with relatively low profit margins (less than ten per cent when times are bad and a percentage in the mid- to high teens when times are good, according to Decherd). Half the Belo stock is owned by family or extended family members and more than seventy per cent of the voting stock is controlled by this group.

The single greatest difference I found between *The News* and other newspapers I have known was the felt presence of ownership values here. Turf battles aren't tolerated at *The Morning News*. Nor is cynicism or whining in columns or features. And there is an age difference of at least ten years between Burl Osborne and Ralph Langer and their heirs apparent, Jeremy Halbreich and Bob Mong. This came through in many ways, and not least in the willingness of employees on the business side of the paper to support a disproportionate amount of new investment in continual product improvements.

In the mid to late 1970s, when the *Times Herald's* Tom Johnson and one of his successors seemed to be making headway in courting Dallas' movers and shakers, Robert Decherd and Jeremy Halbreich immersed themselves in community affairs. At twenty-nine, Decherd became president of the Dallas symphony board, and Halbreich was named a member of the Dallas art museum board. They have served (and continue to serve) on many local boards and commissions since. This allows Osborne and his senior editors to keep some distance from the community so as to avoid real or imagined conflicts of interest.

"Too many newspapers serve only the sixty per cent of their community that their large advertisers are interested in," said newspaper analyst John Morton. "Although it's obviously hard to deliver, hard to collect, hard to serve a part of the market that isn't terribly interested in what you have to say – newspapers owe it to their special position under the First Amendment to try and reach that other thirty to forty per cent."

There are no Dallas neighborhoods to which *The News* refuses to deliver papers (although there are "gray areas" where potential subscribers must pay in advance). By keeping its cover price low and by refusing to curtail delivery that is costly or dangerous or of little use to its advertisers, *The News* has adopted a populist circulation philosophy. By Wall Street's standards, it has adopted a populist pricing philosophy for its advertisers as well.

The question now seems to be whether the newsroom will be able to shift gears and develop more of a bottoms-up philosophy there, whether reporters and first line supervisors will be encouraged to develop to their full potential, and whether women will become, or will feel the environment is right for them to want to become, senior editors with clout. There is already some precedent for such a strategy.

Since the summer of 1994, Ralph Langer and Bob Mong have been meeting with small groups of reporters and first-line editors in the hard news departments. The objective, in Langer's words, is to make sure there's a "shared vision" now that the *Times Herald* is gone; in Mong's, to address rumors with facts and to encourage reporters to go deeper in their writing, to make more connections, and to pay greater attention to context. This probably means more stories will need to be reviewed by senior editors, but both reporters and the newspaper should benefit from the effort, he said.

And in 1987, after the bottom fell out of the Texas real estate and energy markets, *The News* launched an incentive plan aimed at cutting costs, raising revenues, and improving customer service. Twelve hundred employees took part, two-thirds of the company, and more than $4 million in cost savings and additional revenues were generated, double the goal. For the first time, people at the lowest levels were asked for advice, and suddenly, ideas started flowing from the bottom up instead of the top down. "It was like lancing a boil," said controller (now circulation vice president) Barry Peckham, who ran the program. "We hadn't even had a suggestion box before."

A test of how successful *The News* is at being a newspaper for *all* the people will come when the paper raises its daily street price from twenty-five cents to thirty-five or fifty cents. *The News* is one of only four large newspapers in the country that still sells for twenty-five cents on the street. The others are *The Washington Post, St. Petersburg Times,* and the *Star-Ledger* in Newark, New Jersey.

Emotion isn't something Dallas or the people running *The Morning News* have always dealt with very well. In a city built by and for businessmen, problems often need to be presented in a reasoned, logical way. Decorum is important. Often, it is the person confident or sophisticated enough to write the letter or make a phone call who gets heard. People who don't present their arguments in an appropriate way can fail to get their message across.

But democracy is messy, not neat and tidy, not rational and detached. The more participatory life in Dallas becomes, as surely it will, democracy is likely to get messier still.

In its local reporting, will *The News* be willing to tell *all* its readers what is happening, not just those smart or sophisticated enough to read between the lines? Or those patient enough and with time enough to read through the mass of facts *The News* still tends to throw at its projects and big stories? Will editors allow or encourage their reporters to synthesize, to say what something means early enough in a story so readers won't be tempted to stop reading?

Two recent enterprise stories by architecture critic David Dillon that senior editors were proud of, and that went through several drafts and revisions before appearing in the paper, were titled "Security for sale: Gated communities prosper in fearful society; critics say they foster segregation, isolation"; and "Safe havens: Gated communities are appealing to today's yearning for security."

The main story started on page one and ran for eighty inches, and the accompanying story ran for sixty-two inches. The main story began:

"A familiar sound in American cities and suburbs these days is the clanging gate. Not the garden gate, or the alley gate, but the gate that closes off the street, the block and increasingly the entire neighborhood.

"Worried about crime and property values and skeptical of government's ability to do much about either, an estimated four million Americans now live in gated communities. . . .

"One third of all new communities in Southern California are gated. The percentages are similar in Phoenix, the suburbs of Washington, D.C., and in many parts of Florida.

"New home sales in large master-planned communities such as Irving's Los Colinas . . . rose seventeen per cent in 1992, with Texas accounting for one-fifth of the national total."

The accompanying story began:

"Promoted as the latest advance in luxury living, gated communities date back at least to the Middle Ages and the Renaissance. Princes built them to shelter their families and loyal retainers in times of siege and pestilence, often surrounding them with towers, moats, and drawbridges."

The problem was that it wasn't until deep into this second story that readers get to the question of how effective these gated communities are in curtailing crime.

"Security experts generally agree that gates and walls keep out peeping toms, hub cap thieves and other forms of 'transient crime'. . . . But the effectiveness of gates in preventing serious crime is more questionable. Rick Highfill, division president of Protective Services in Irving, points out that many security companies pay guards little more than minimum wage, which can translate into low morale, poor training and a turnover rate of two hundred per cent a year. Even at ten dollars an hour, a low figure, the annual cost for twenty-four-hour security covering one gate and one guard is $87,000. Which is why many guardhouses are unoccupied after dark, a dummy camera and bogus warning signs take the place of patrols.

" 'Security is more perception than reality,' adds Frank Zaccanelli, executive vice president of the Perot Group's Hillwood Development Corporation. 'If a professional thief wants to break in, he'll find a way.

But people perceive gated communities to be more secure, and from a developer's point of view that's a more marketable commodity.' "

The News, which now prides itself on setting the agenda for *all* its readers, still seemed reluctant to challenge its wealthiest constituency.

Osborne has said that in a city with just one daily newspaper, the old adage that a newspaper's job is to comfort the afflicted and afflict the comfortable may be out-of-date. A newspaper's role now needs to be more that of an honest broker – a place, sometimes the only place, where all voices in a city or region can meet and be heard.

That sounds fine so long as the newspaper isn't perceived as paternal, and so long as all voices get to be heard in a fair and easy-to-understand way. In the past, *The News* has tended to focus on what people have in common rather than on what serves to divide them. Yet often it is unacknowledged differences that cause the problems.

Robert Decherd's office across the street from *The Morning News* building has floor-to-ceiling windows which offer a spectacular view of downtown Dallas. But otherwise in the large, airy room there is little to reveal the man except for two winged lions on his bookshelf – one inscribed to Robert, the other to his father, both given in recognition for having served as chairman of the board of trustees at the St. Mark's school. In a far corner that visitors seldom approach hangs a framed quotation by Teddy Roosevelt.

"It is not the critic who counts . . . not the man who points out how the strong man stumbles. . . . The credit belongs to the man actually in the arena, whose face is marred by dust and sweat."

Decherd blushes when asked about the quotation. "It was given by a friend. I felt honor bound to hang it. It certainly isn't anything I go around reciting. I couldn't get six of its words in their proper order if I tried." But then he stops himself and grins and says, "Well yes, I do agree with the spirit of the thing."

Decherd is forty-three, with twenty-two years before retirement. His son was recently named editor of the middle school paper at

St. Mark's. The only other family member in the business is James Moroney III, who oversees Belo's television stations under Ward Huey. Decherd would like to see a fifth-generation family member run the company one day. His perspective is long term.

He sees Dallas and *The Morning News*, perhaps like himself, as still in their early adulthood, not yet at peak potential or fully mature. He says as we approach the twenty-first century, Americans "are engaged in an unprecedented undertaking: constructing the first multiracial, multi-ethnic, multi-religious democracy in history." He blames network television for abandoning wholesome, mass appeal viewing, yet in 1994 bought two more network affiliates, in New Orleans and Seattle. He had hoped that by now his company would have acquired another mid- to large-size newspaper, but so far none has been available. He says that he and Osborne are gambling that *The News* can hold on to the many talented people it has stockpiled by continuing to improve and expand.

"Once having reached distinction, it's a more difficult management task having to sustain it. We're holding ourselves up to a higher standard now, in many ways an abstraction."

And how does this challenge get communicated to the rank and file?

"By force of personality," Decherd said. "And in Burl Osborne we've got the best man in the country for that."

Since his kidney transplant twenty-eight years ago, Osborne has lived each day as if it might be his last. He has told those closest to him he hadn't expected to live this long. They say it is this quality which helps to explain his extraordinary drive and energy. Shortly before this book went to press, Osborne had a second kidney transplant, this time with an organ donated by his brother. The kidney donated by his mother in 1966 had begun to fail. The second operation was also a success.

Robert Decherd said recently that *The News*, in this its second incarnation, is almost totally the product of Osborne's "magical instincts." He wanted the story of how Burl transformed the newspaper to be told.

ACKNOWLEDGMENTS

Most of the information in this book is based on interviews and observation. So it was crucial that I have easy access to whomever and whatever seemed pertinent.

I am particularly grateful to Burl Osborne and Robert Decherd, who made sure that no obstacles were put in my path, and who answered whatever questions I put to them; also to Ralph Langer and Jeremy Halbreich who did the same, and allowed me unfettered entree to their people and work spaces.

Most of the people I talked with at *The News* are mentioned in the text, and to these, and whomever I may have missed, I say thanks for your patience and good-natured assistance. A special thanks to Judy Sall in the reference department who gave me a place to hang my hat and helped me find answers to questions when few others could; to Bob Yates who guided me through the sports department when Dave Smith was out of town; to Ben McConnell, Ed Kohorst, and John Cranfill, who taught me the subtleties of graphics; to George Stone and Barbara Wells in research who opened their files to me; to Barry Boesch, the guru of zoned editions; to Michele Medley and Judith Garrett who helped to put the history and culture of the newspaper in better perspective; and to Ricki Conway, Amy Keepes, Judy Stafford, Audrey Bolling, and Judy Metcalf who responded to my many requests with good humor.

I am grateful to Jack Finefrock, Tony Gloeggler, Alfred Eckes, Andraya Kulinyi, and Phil Brown, who read various parts or versions of my manuscript and offered many helpful suggestions on construction and content; to Susan Williamson at Philadelphia's Annenberg School of Communications who helped me decide that *The News* was the newspaper I wanted to profile; to Dr. John H. Murphy at the University of Texas who gave me a copy of his study and video on *The News'* competitive history; and to John Ware, my agent and friend, who put me in touch with Alexia Dorsnyski, who had been looking for someone to do a book like this and who for over a year gave it her best effort; to Frances Vick who rescued the project after Alexia was forced to withdraw, and who embraced the concept of visuals; and to Charlotte M. Wright, my new editor, who also had many helpful suggestions.

Responsibility for the book's contents, however, is soley mine.

In addition to those mentioned above, I talked with and wish to thank: Richie Adubato, William E. Ahearn, Joe Belden, Scott Bennett, Lou Boccardi, Roy E. Bode, Richard Blum, Richard Brettell, Terri Burke, John Buzzetta, Adelfa B. Callejo, Carlton Carl, Reese Cleghorn, Richard L. Conner, W. A. Criswell, Jim Crupi, Bill Cryer, Lee Cullum, Rich Dalrymple, Joe M. Dealey, Michael Duggan, Thomas M. Dunning, Peter Elkind, Jack Evans, Peter Falco, Leonard Forman, Joseph Forsee, Domingo Garcia, Lupe Garcia, Yolette Garcia, Robert H. Giles, Barbara Renaud Gonzalez, Sharon Grigsby, Marty Haag, Buster Haas, Jan Hart, Tom Hays, Thomas J. Holbein, Zan Holmes, Melissa Houtte, Ward L. Huey Jr., Jodie C. Hughes, Will D. Jarrett, Lee Jackson, Jimmy Johnson, Tom Johnson, Alex S. Jones, Timothy M. Kelly, Ellen Kampinsky, James C. Lagier, David T. Lane, Michael R. Levy, John Lumpkin, Melinda Machado, René Martinez, Maxwell E. McCombs, Gordon Medinica, Mary Jo Meisner, Rodger Meier, James M. Moroney Jr., John Morton, Ken Noble, Betty Osborne, Judy Polumbaum, Robert G. Picard, John Wiley Price, John A. Rector Jr., Edward T. Rincon, Gene Roberts, Matilda Robinson, Robert Rose, Bob Ray Sanders, John Seigenthaler, George Shafer, Merrie Spaeth, Tom Simmons, Jean Simmons, Monica Smith, William Solomon, Steve Star, Wick Temple, Charles T. Terrell, States D. Tompkins, Marvin Veal, Paul Watler, Perry Williams and Roy Williams.

BIBLIOGRAPHY

I relied mostly on interviews and observation, but also on the following books and articles for background and reference.

Acheson, Sam. *35,000 Days in Texas*. New York: Macmillan, 1938.

Auletta, Ken. *Three Blind Mice: How the TV Networks Lost Their Way.* New York: Vintage, 1992.

Bagdikian, Ben. *The Media Monopoly; A Startling Report on the 50 Corporations That Control What America Sees, Hears and Reads.* Boston: Beacon Press, 1983.

Bayless, Skip. *The Boys*. New York: Pocket Books, 1993.

Bissinger, H. G. *Friday Night Lights: A Town, a Team, and a Dream.* New York: HarperCollins, 1990.

Bogart, Leo. *Press and Public: Who Reads, What, When, Where, and Why in American Newspapers.* Hillsdale, New Jersey: Lawrence Erlbaum Associates, 1989.

Crouse, Timothy. *The Boys on the Bus*. New York: Ballantine, 1973.

Elkind, Peter. "The Legacy of Citizen Robert." *Texas Monthly* (July, 1985).

Greene, A. C. *Dallas USA*. Austin: Texas Monthly Press, 1984.

Holley, Joe. "Confronting La Frontera." *Columbia Journalism Review* (May/June 1994).

Ivins, Molly. *Molly Ivins Can't Say That, Can She?* New York: Random House, 1991.

Martin A. and Solomon, Norman. *Unreliable Sources: A Guide to Detecting Bias in News Media.* New York: Lyle Stuart, 1990.

Osborne, Burl, and others. *Readers: How To Gain Readers and Retain Them.* New York: Newspaper Advertising Bureau, 1983.

Payne, Darwin. *Big D: Triumphs and Troubles of an American Supercity in the 20th Century.* Dallas: Three Forks Press, 1994.

Picard, Robert G., Maxwell E. McCombs and others. *Press Concentration and Monopoly: New Perspectives on Newspaper Ownership and Operation.* Norwood, New Jersey: Ablex, 1988.

Schutze, Jim. *The Accommodation: The Politics of Race in an American City.* Secaucus, New Jersey: Citadel Press, 1986.

Schutze Jim. "It Wasn't Murder. Was it Suicide?": How the *Times Herald* Died." *D* (February, 1992).

Sharpe, Ernest. *G. B. Dealey of the Dallas News.* New York: Henry Holt and Co., 1955.

Smith, Griffin, Jr. "Texas Newspapers: BA-A-A-D." *Texas Monthly* (June 1974).

Squires, James D. *Read All About It: The Corporate Takeover of America's Newspapers.* New York: Times Books, 1993.

Trillin, Calvin. "American Chronicles: The Life and Times of Joe Bob Briggs, So Far." *The New Yorker* (December 22, 1986).

GLOSSARY

ABC: the Audit Bureau of Circulation, the independent organization
    that compiles circulation statistics.

Advance: a story previewing an event such as a concert or election that
    is about to happen.

Advertorial: a positive story with similar subject matter, positioned near
    or next to advertising copy. Not to be confused with a straight news
    story.

Agate: very small type, normally used for box scores in sports, and in
    classified advertising.

Beat: the subject area assigned to a reporter, such as the police beat.

Bulldog: the newspaper's first Sunday edition, usually available as early
    as noon Saturday.

Byline: the name of the reporter who wrote the story, as it appears at
    the beginning of the story.

Circulation: in print, the number of copies sold or distributed; in
    broadcast, the number of households tuning to a station in a week's
    time; in outdoor advertising, the number of cars passing a billboard in
    a month.

Classified Advertising: advertising located in one specific part of the
    paper in which products and services are grouped by classifications.
    Within each classification, categories are broken down even further so
    that a reader can easily find what he or she wants.

Collect run: a method of doubling the number of pages that can be
    printed in a single press run. The method allows the newspaper to
    handle more advertising or special news coverage, but it slows down
    the presses and takes longer to the edition, requiring earlier
    deadlines.

Composing room: a room next to the newsroom where the different
    elements of the paper are assembled prior to being sent to the
    printing plant.

Crop: to eliminate portions of the copy, usually on a photograph.

Cutline: the words under a photograph that explain further what is happening. At *The Morning News*, cutlines are written by the photographer who took the picture.

Double truck: a full two-page layout, either in news or advertising.

Enterprise: a story, photograph, or graphic not pegged to a breaking news event. Usually something that wouldn't have been done without unusual initiative.

Facts Box: information that can be pulled out of a story and presented in a sidebar for reading at a glance.

Feature: a story emphasizing its human interest or entertainment aspects.

Fly: when late changes are made to an edition "on the fly" after the presses start rolling.

JOA (Joint Operating Agreement): an arrangement where the business operations of a morning and evening newspaper are combined, while the two newsrooms continue to operate separately and compete. A way to maintain the semblance of a two-newspaper city in an era when more large evening newspapers are going out of business.

Jump: the continuation of a story from one page, usually a section front, to another page inside.

Morgue: (called the reference department at *The Morning News*); the place where the back files, photographs, and instructions on how to access data bases are kept.

National Advertising (or General Advertising): advertising placed by national companies or those based in other cities than the paper's parent city.

Newshole: the space in the paper allotted to news stories, as opposed to advertising.

Newsprint: rough, inexpensive paper made mostly from groundwood pulp and small amounts of chemical pulp, used for printing newspapers.

Obituary or obit: a story reporting a person's death.

Op Ed or Viewpoints page: the page opposite the page where the editorials run.

Overrun: copies printed in excess of the normal press run.

Preprints: full color rotogravure or offset material not printed on newspaper presses. Printed in advance and shipped to be inserted with the regular press run.

Press run: total number of copies printed.

Projects editor: the person who supervises enterprise and investigative reporting.

Pull quote: a design element constructed by extracting a compelling quote from a story, setting it in large type and inserting the quote in the text.

Puff: a publicity release praising an individual, company or organization, usually of little or no news value.

Retail advertising: advertising placed by local merchants.

ROP or full run: short for "run of paper." News or ads that the newspaper prints itself (unlike preprints), and which run in the paper's full circulation (as opposed to just a zoned edition).

Sacred cow: a person or institution that constantly gets favorable and/or heavy news treatment, regardless of the merits.

Sidebar: a story that highlights one aspect of a larger story and appears alongside it on the page.

Shopper: a free distribution newspaper, usually filled with ads, but with very little news content.

Stand alone section: a section not connected to any other part of the newspaper.

Straight run: running the presses twice as fast as in a collect run, in the interest of including late sports scores and getting the paper delivered to homes and newsstands earlier. In a straight run you are restricted to the number of sections you can print. As a result, some sections may be printed in advance.

Stringer: a part-time reporter normally living outside the newspaper's normal coverage area.

Summary blurb: a succinct synopsis displayed beneath the headline to provide additional information to readers, particularly skimmers.

Tabloid: a newspaper half the size of a regular newspaper, such as *The Morning News*' Guide section.

TMC (Total Market Coverage): a special section or sections delivered to subscribing newspaper households and mailed to non-subscribing households to achieve total coverage of an area.

Typeface: a single design for letters, numerals and other characters.

Typo: a typographical error.

Universal desk: a desk that handles copy from several different departments.

We prints: standard-size, as distinct from tabloid-size, advertising sections which run as part of the regular paper.

Zoning: printing and distributing news and/or advertising copy for a part of a newspaper's circulation area.

INDEX

91, 195; founding, 18–19; legal
issues, 13, 100–104; minority
awareness, 12, 125, 135, 136–
39, 160–61, 161–69, 176, 181;
newsroom, 12, 31, 160;
ownership, 7–8; personnel, 12,
13, 16–27, 64, 81; philosophies,
7, 33, 36, 37, 48–49, 72, 86, 124;
photographs, 32, 33–34, 41, 54,
58, 67, 74, 81, 82, 120, 123, 187;
policies, 57–58, 59, 85, 90, 102,
117, 129; production, 53, 54;
readers, 49, 59, 155, 174, 180–
81; sponsorships, 111, 143;
traditions, 13, 19. *See also*
individual sections
Dallas Museum of Art, 116, 161
Dallas Observer, 15, 94, 127,
156–57, 161, 175, 185–86
Dallas Police Association, 52, 53,
135
Dallas Times Herald, 17, 21, 23,
25, 35, 39, 40, 49, 53, 62, 93–94,
124, 125, 153–58, 164, 166, 169;
advertising, 21, 85, 117, 119;
circulation, 7, 21, 72, 83;
closing, 13, 14, 143–52, 180;
final edition, 14, 149; lawsuits,
14; ownership, 7; philosophies,
70; proposals, 146
Davidson, John, 41, 58, 74, 81, 82,
187
Dayton Journal, 26
Dealey, E. M. (Ted), 8, 19, 21
Dealey, George Bannerman, 7, 8,
13, 18–19, 21, 22, 31, 61, 177

Dealey, Joe, Jr., 19, 20, 21, 24, 62,
90
Dealey, Joe, Sr., 21
Decherd, Ben, 17, 20
Decherd, Maureen Healey, 19
Decherd, Robert, 8, 9, 14, 17–25,
34, 40, 43, 44, 61, 71, 85, 87, 90,
109, 126, 129, 144, 145, 148,
151, 154, 155, 156–57, 158, 173–
74, 177–78, 188, 190, 191,
199–200
Decker, Susan, 190–91
Denver Post, 145
DeOre, Bill, 89–90
Des Moines Register (The), 15
Detroit Free Press, 12, 158
Detroit News (The), 60
Dillon, David, 44, 197
Discoveries section, 33, 34
Dowd, Maureen, 179
Dufner, Ed, 47
Dunn, Jerry, 53
Dunne, John, 106
Dyer, Eileen, 117

Edgar, Mark, 92
editorial pages, 36–38, 86, 89,
127, 154, 173–74
editors, 45–49, 51–52, 56–57, 58,
160, 163, 168, 176, 192, 196
Education Extra, 56
Eig, Jonathan, 115
election coverage, 38–39, 47, 54,
58–59, 61, 67–70, 92–93,
135–36, 143, 178–80
Elkind, Peter, 157, 161